Applying Models-based Practice in Physical Education

This book is a concise, practical introduction to Models-based Practice (MbP), a transformative approach to physical education and sport pedagogy that uses multiple pedagogical models in the design and delivery of physical education programs.

The book introduces the core concepts underpinning the MbP approach – including models such as teaching games for understanding, sport education, cooperative learning and health-based physical education – and examines its significance for teaching, learning, curriculum and assessment. With an emphasis on evidence-based practice and student learning, and full of practical tips and features to encourage critical thinking, the book explains how to develop successful, flexible and sustainable MbP programs that can deliver real educational and health and well-being benefits for children and young people, in schools or in after-school or community-based settings.

Applying Models-based Practice in Physical Education is intended for current and prospective teachers of physical education who are responsible for organising and enacting programs at all grade levels. It will also be of interest to researchers, students and other sport pedagogy practitioners, such as coaches who are looking for new and innovative ways of working with children and young people.

Ashley Casey is Professor of Physical Education and Pedagogy at Loughborough University, a National Teaching Fellow and Series Editor of the Routledge Focus on Sport Pedagogy.

David Kirk is Professor of Education at the University of Strathclyde and Editor of the Routledge journal *Physical Education and Sport Pedagogy*.

Routledge Focus on Sport Pedagogy
Series editor: Ash Casey
Loughborough University, UK

The field of sport pedagogy (physical education and coaching) is united by the desire to improve the experiences of young people and adult participants. The *Routledge Focus on Sport Pedagogy* series presents small books on big topics in an effort to eradicate the boundaries that currently exist between young people, adult learners, coaches, teachers and academics, in schools, clubs and universities. Theoretically grounded but with a strong emphasis on practice, the series aims to open up important and useful new perspectives on teaching, coaching and learning in sport and physical education.

Pedagogies of Social Justice in Physical Education and Youth Sport
Shrehan Lynch, Jennifer L. Walton-Fisette and Carla Luguetti

Learner-Oriented Teaching and Assessment in Youth Sport
Edited by Cláudio Farias and Isabel Mesquita

Physical Education Pedagogies for Health
Edited by Lorraine Cale and Jo Harris

Flipped Learning in Physical Education
Opportunities and Applications
Ove Østerlie, Chad Killian and Julia Sargent

Teaching Disabled Children in Physical Education
(Dis)connections between Research and Practice
Anthony J. Maher and Justin A. Haegele

Applying Models-based Practice in Physical Education
Ashley Casey and David Kirk

For more information about this series, please visit: www.routledge.com/Routledge-Focus-on-Sport-Pedagogy/book-series/RFSPED

Applying Models-based Practice in Physical Education

Ashley Casey and David Kirk

LONDON AND NEW YORK

First published 2024
by Routledge
4 Park Square, Milton Park, Abingdon, Oxon OX14 4RN

and by Routledge
605 Third Avenue, New York, NY 10158

Routledge is an imprint of the Taylor & Francis Group, an informa business

© 2024 Ashley Casey and David Kirk

The right of Ashley Casey and David Kirk to be identified as authors of this work has been asserted in accordance with sections 77 and 78 of the Copyright, Designs and Patents Act 1988.

All rights reserved. No part of this book may be reprinted or reproduced or utilised in any form or by any electronic, mechanical, or other means, now known or hereafter invented, including photocopying and recording, or in any information storage or retrieval system, without permission in writing from the publishers.

Trademark notice: Product or corporate names may be trademarks or registered trademarks, and are used only for identification and explanation without intent to infringe.

British Library Cataloguing-in-Publication Data
A catalogue record for this book is available from the British Library

Library of Congress Cataloging-in-Publication Data
Names: Casey, Ashley, author. | Kirk, David, 1958– author.
Title: Applying models-based practice in physical education / Ashley Casey and David Kirk.
Description: Abingdon, Oxon ; New York, NY : Routledge, 2024. | Series: Routledge focus on sport pedagogy | Includes bibliographical references and index.
Identifiers: LCCN 2024014954 (print) | LCCN 2024014955 (ebook) | ISBN 9780367365561 (hardback) | ISBN 9781032822488 (paperback) | ISBN 9780429347078 (ebook)
Subjects: LCSH: Physical education and training—Study and teaching. | Physical education for children. | Sports for children.
Classification: LCC GV361 .C289 2024 (print) | LCC GV361 (ebook) | DDC 796.07—dc23/eng/20240409
LC record available at https://lccn.loc.gov/2024014954
LC ebook record available at https://lccn.loc.gov/2024014955

ISBN: 978-0-367-36556-1 (hbk)
ISBN: 978-1-032-82248-8 (pbk)
ISBN: 978-0-429-34707-8 (ebk)

DOI: 10.4324/9780429347078

Typeset in Times New Roman
by Apex CoVantage, LLC

Ash and David:

Dedicated to the teachers whose unwavering commitment to the children in their care gives this book its purpose. Special appreciation to our colleagues, PhD students and fellow researchers whose vision and dedication to a better physical education provide the rich material for this book. Finally, thanks to Dr Lars Bjørke, whose 'above and beyond' consideration of the final draft helped us to elevate the book and bring it over the line and whose foreword provides such a compelling opening to this work.

Ash: To Sarah, Thomas and Maddie,

In the warmth of your love and unwavering support, this work finds its inspiration. Thank you for the laughter, shared dreams and countless moments that have defined our journey together.

Contents

List of Tables x
List of Figures xi
Foreword xii

1 **What is models-based practice?** 1
  Terminology 3
  Why change traditional practice in physical education? 4
  Why Models-based Practice? 6
  What is a pedagogical model? 8
    The structure of pedagogical models:
      practice architectures 9
    Practice architecture: sayings, doings, relatings 11
  Conclusion 12

2 **What pedagogical models exist?** 14
  Established pedagogical models 14
    Sport education 15
    Teaching games in physical education 15
    Cooperative learning 16
    Teaching personal and social responsibility 17
    Summary 18
    Emerging pedagogical models 18
    Activist pedagogical model for working with girls 18
    Socially vulnerable youth pedagogical model 19
    Health-based physical education pedagogical
      model 20
    Practising pedagogical model 21
  Spectrum of teaching styles 22
    Conclusion 23

3 Preparing to succeed with MbP 27
Playing the long game 27
The groundwork 28
  Learning to teach and learning to learn in new ways 29
  Building the foundations 42
  What are the practice architectures in your school/department? 42
  The sequencing of pedagogical models in MbP 44
Conclusion 46

4 Working collectively and collaboratively: A little help from your friends 49
The importance of collaboration and collective effort when implementing Models-based Practice in physical education 49
Building a shared vision and understanding of MbP among educators 50
Establishing a collaborative culture within the school or department 52
Collaborative problem-solving and troubleshooting to address challenges and barriers 54
Engaging in professional learning communities and networks to support implementation 56
Involving students in the process through student voice and empowerment 56
Reflecting on collective progress and making adjustments based on feedback and evidence 60
Celebrating successes and recognising the contributions of all stakeholders in the implementation of MbP 61
Conclusion 62

5 Making a case for MbP at school level 64
Introduction 64
Stakeholders 65
Reconnaissance 66
The generation of evidence 67
Conclusion 70

6 Conclusion 71
Introduction 71
Transformation through MbP 71
Multiple pedagogical models 72
Embracing change and challenges 72
Collaborative approach 73
Advocacy and evidence-based practice 73
An invitation 73

Index 75

Tables

3.1 Aligning your focus to the chosen model 44

Figures

1.1	The process of model development (Casey & Kirk, 2021, p. 29) (Jewett & Bain, 1995) [Processes of reconsideration added by Casey (2016, p. 59)]	8
3.1	A practice architecture of a pedagogical model	31
3.2	A practice architecture of the practising model	32
3.3	A practice architecture of sport education	33
3.4	A practice architecture of TGFU	34
3.5	A practice architecture of TPSR	35
3.6	A practice architecture of the activist model	36
3.7	A practice architecture of health-based physical education	37
3.8	A practice architecture of cooperative learning	38
3.9	A multi-activity approach to the 11–12-year-olds' curriculum	45
3.10	The use of two models in a multi-activity 11–12-year-olds' curriculum	46
4.1	A practice architecture of the practising model	52
4.2	Student comment card	57

Foreword

I assume, since you have opted to read this book, that you agree that physical education has the potential to equip young people with the competencies they need to live good lives and flourish as moving human beings. I also believe many of you agree that physical education could play an even more important role in the lives of all young people, and that re-thinking why, what and how physical education matters is important.

Working previously as a primary school physical education teacher in Norway for several years, I was aware of the limitations of my homogeneous sports-dominated 'do-as-I-do' pedagogy and recognised the need for change. Yet, I did not. Not out of bad will or lack of ambition but due to what I perceived then as a lack of available suggestions for how I could 'do physical education better' for my students and I felt kind of captured within the boundaries of my own practices. Learning about Models-based Practice over the last decade has therefore been a revelation for me. Models-based Practice has allowed me to crawl out of the rabbit hole I've found myself in and explore new perspectives, ideas and practices for physical education. Being a teacher educator today, I acknowledge that Models-based Practice has also allowed me to challenge future- and in-service teachers thinking around why physical education is important, what young people should learn and how physical education can be taught so that it supports what they as teachers are trying to achieve. For this, I particularly say to Ash and David a huge 'thank you' for their work on Models-based Practice – a gratitude that extends to this book.

Although Models-based Practice has been a 'talked about future' for physical education for years, it has not to the same extent been 'actioned.' I believe one key explanation for this is that scholarship so far has emphasised arguing theoretically for why, what and how Models-based Practice is a good idea – and less about why, what and how Models-based Practice could be applied to practice. Hence, I believe this book, with its emphasis on applying, is a much-needed and significant contribution for practitioners who are ready for change but do not really know where to start or what steps they could take next – much like I felt years ago. Throughout this book the authors provide suggestions for everyone, regardless of where you are in the process of adopting a

Models-based Practice, on what possible actions you could take next. However, as strongly emphasised by the authors, Models-based Practice is not something that merely exists, but is something that you, as a professional and educated practitioner with specific knowledge about your local context, create, develop and refine together with you students. So, in reading this book I challenge you to consider: What will my first action with my students be? Why so? When and where will that happen?

Being someone who genuinely believes that Models-based Practice can transform physical education for the better for young people, it is a pleasure to see a book taking the field one step further. Good reading.

Dr Lars Bjørke
Inland Norway University of Applied Sciences
December 2023

1 What is models-based practice?

The idea of an approach to physical education based on models originated in the USA and has been around since at least the 1980s (see Jewett & Bain, 1985; Metzler, 2000). It offers an alternative way of thinking about how to construct physical education programs. While this idea has been circulating in the physical education and sport pedagogy research literature for some time, it has yet to gain traction in practice, for reasons we will explore later in this chapter.

Despite the apparent lack of traction, we strongly believe that a models-based approach offers a different and better future for physical education. As you will note as you read further, we have been strongly influenced by work from the USA. That said, we are also critical of some aspects of this work. Indeed, our own take on this approach is seen in what we have termed Models-based Practice (MbP).

'Practice' is a key term and refers to what is done on the ground in physical education programs, in terms of both planning for and enacting physical education in schools and related pedagogical settings (such as after-school and some community-based programs). The term 'models-based' describes this practice. The models we have in mind are pedagogical models. Some of these you may have heard of and perhaps have used yourself, such as teaching games for understanding, sport education and cooperative learning, among others. Equally others, such as health-based physical education (HbPE) or the practising model, may be new to you and yet may be one of the approaches you may bring into your practice because of your reading of this book.

> Models are becoming increasingly well-known in physical education. They are taught in many undergraduate and postgraduate courses and feature in most teacher development events. Worryingly, however, Sport Education, Teaching Games for Understanding and other capitalised models have started to represent a single way of teaching.

DOI: 10.4324/9780429347078-1

2 What Is Models-based Practice?

> In much the same way that Sellotape (UK) and Scotch Tape (USA and Canada) have come to represent all sticky tapes, so capitalised models have come to represent *the* way of using Sport Education (for example). This simply isn't possible. While every model has a main idea, some critical elements, learning aspirations and pedagogical characteristics, no model is used in the same way in two different schools. Instead, local adaptations are made to suit the context and young people to be taught. As such we use lowercase in this book to position sport education (for example) as a pedagogical act which is bespoke to a single site and not a blueprint to be placed in every physical education program (for a fuller explanation, see Casey et al., 2021).

The word 'pedagogy' is also important in our approach and is worth defining. We see pedagogy as the interaction and interdependence of teaching, learning, curriculum and assessment. Since these four elements of pedagogy interact, when we change one, there is a knock-on effect on the others. They are also interdependent in the sense that they are impossible to pull apart and practice by themselves. We may focus on one element for analysis purposes, by bringing it into the foreground, but the others will always be there in the background. Therefore, when we write about *pedagogical* models, we hold that these models contain all four of these elements together.

Finally, the word 'model' is also used in a specific way in MbP and has several connotations. We write about models in the sense that they are multidimensional and multi-faceted approaches to physical education. They not only contain the four elements of pedagogy but also will have embedded in them the resources required to implement them, the characteristics of the teachers and learners who will use and experience them, and the range of contexts in which they may be appropriate educational tools.

We also write about models in the sense that they are not programs in themselves but, rather, sets of rules and guidelines for the creation of local programs in specific schools and other sites. In this way they should be considered as balls of clay to be moulded rather than prefabricated buildings which are flat-packed off-site and assembled on campus. We use a specialised term to describe this feature of pedagogical models, which is that they are 'design specifications.' We will come back to this issue in a short while.

We wrote above that the idea of models-based approaches to physical education has been around since at least the 1980s but has yet to gain traction. How can this be, you might ask, given pedagogical models such as teaching games for understanding, sport education and cooperative learning have also been around for decades?

There are two ways to answer this question. The first is that when these popular and well-known models were first conceived and practised in physical education, they were not described as pedagogical models and did not have the identifiable structure that we argue pedagogical models require. Again, we use a specialised term for this structure: 'practice architecture' (which we explore later in this chapter). Suffice to say in answer to the question, the idea that these popular approaches to physical education could be viewed as pedagogical models came decades after their creation, though some were described as instructional models (Metzler, 2000) and curriculum models (Lund & Tannehill, 2014).

The second answer is that while popular approaches such as sport education and teaching games for understanding have been practised by physical educators for many years, this has typically been as a single model, not as a part of an MbP. Furthermore, these alternative approaches have most often been 'parachuted into' traditional physical education programs rather than replacing them. In contrast, when we use the term 'MbP,' we are referring to the use of multiple models to create and organise whole physical education programs.

Thus, it is the case that while physical educators have implemented single pedagogical models in their programs over the past 30 to 40 years, they have rarely (at least rarely in terms of what is recorded in the research literature) used multiple pedagogical models to engage in MbP. Indeed, there are so few examples recorded of MbP that it remains for all intents and purposes an aspiration for physical education rather than a fact. We believe, nevertheless, that it is an idea that is, as Lawrence Stenhouse would have it, worth putting to the test of practice.

Terminology

A range of different terminology associated with models-based approaches has emerged over time. For someone new to this idea, and even for a more experienced reader, these differences can be confusing. The terminology we use in this book, as we have just explained, is Models-based Practice (MbP). How does this relate to the other terminology you will encounter in the literature concerned with models-based approaches?

You will see a range of other terminology in the research literature and in textbooks. For example, although Jewett and Bain (1985) took a models-based approach to physical education that has been very influential in informing our thinking, they favoured the term 'curriculum model.' Metzler (2000, 2011, 2017), on the other hand, prefers the notion of instructional models and writes about Model-Based Instruction. Some authors, such as Dyson et al. (2016), claim that curriculum models involve longer-term planning, while instructional models focus on more micro-unit and lesson levels. But they

4 *What Is Models-based Practice?*

also claim that some models can be both curriculum *and* instructional models. Recently, Dyson et al. (2021) have written about Models-Based Practices such as sport education and teaching games for understanding.

We find this proliferation of terminology and the apparent inconsistencies of explanation and use of terms unhelpful, particularly when we are working with teachers. Teachers quite reasonably ask, are these different approaches to physical education that are being proposed? And how do they relate to the terminology of Models-based Practice and pedagogical models that we use?

While this range of terms appears to signal a lack of consensus among scholars and advocates of models-based approaches, we think there is more agreement than difference. Even though Metzler (2000) writes about Model-Based Instruction (with the singular 'model'), a careful study of his book shows he is, like us, referring to the use of multiple models to construct and constitute physical education programs. Despite differences in terminology, we have learnt much from Metzler's approach and incorporate many of his ideas in MbP.

Before we consider the case that might be put in support of adopting MbP, it's important to have a sense of why traditional practice in physical education may not be fit for purpose.

Why change traditional practice in physical education?

We believe MbP offers the opportunity to open a universe of possibilities regarding the educational and health and well-being benefits children and young people might derive from their participation in well-designed and implemented physical education programs. The research literature on the uses of pedagogical models provides us with glimpses of what might be possible.

We also believe that physical education in its current and dominant form is failing to realise these benefits. Before supporting this claim, it's worth considering two, of many, current and popular justifications for physical education in the school curriculum. We think both have considerable value, but as justifications also have serious limitations in relation to the traditionally dominant approach.

The first of these, which dates back to at least the post–World War II period in Britain and to slightly different times elsewhere, is that physical education provides children and young people with the skills and dispositions to lead a physically active life. It does this through providing a broad and balanced curriculum which gives students experiences of a wide range of physical activities so that they might choose which of these they will pursue into adulthood.

This justification explains, in part, why traditional physical education programs tend to be organised around categories of physical activities such as games, aquatics, gymnastics, dance and outdoor pursuits. It also explains why they tend to be made up of short units of these games and sports in the hope that, by introducing students to a broad range of activities, they will hopefully

What Is Models-based Practice? 5

find something they enjoy and will do for the rest of their lives. In the USA this justification and its resultant forms of practice are often described as the multi-activity curriculum. This justification is so commonplace and widespread that it is hard for us to ascribe it to any particular author(s).

A second and somewhat more recent justification, dating from the late 1980s and early 1990s, is that physical education is a basis for managing risk factors such as sedentariness that contribute to obesity and cardiovascular disease. This too is a commonplace justification for physical education in schools, though we can attribute it to a particular group of researchers and advocates, represented, for instance, by Sallis and McKenzie (1991), who argued that physical education should be considered as a key contribution to public health strategy.

In contrast to the first justification, this risk-management justification for physical education tends to result in a narrowing of the range of physical activities included in the curriculum. Applying the notion of Moderate to Vigorous Physical Activity (MVPA), supporters of this public health approach argue that whatever activity is underway in a lesson, it should ideally be carried out with MVPA in mind.

We think you will recognise both justifications. The former appears to us to remain the most favoured among physical educators. While widely cited in policy documents, the latter, risk-management, approach seems to have had limited influence on practice, evidenced in McKenzie and Lounsbery's (2009) disappointed conclusion that physical education was 'the pill not taken,' belying the 'exercise-is-medicine' logic of this orientation.

Both justifications are appropriate, as far as they go. It is the practice that supports them that we consider to be problematic. For instance, in terms of the multi-activity approach associated with the first justification, the relationship between what happens in lessons and the learning aspirations set for students rarely aligns. Often, a range of learning aspirations are stated, drawing on cognitive, physical, social and affective domains, while also citing health benefits and outcomes. These weighty expectations for learning often rest on practices that are, for most of the lesson time, focused on learning decontextualised techniques of particular games and sports.

Please note that we do not blame teachers for the widespread use of this multi-activity, sport-technique-based form of physical education. Nor are we saying that the two reasons above are wrong; we simply believe that they only capture a small part of all the good reasons for doing physical education. Indeed, given the ways in which time and space are employed to organise the school's activities, through the timetable and the 'classroom,' multi-activity, sport-technique-based form of physical education is a logical response. In secondary schools, in particular, the two or three 50-minute periods of physical education sprinkled through the school week, with the constant changing of subjects and classrooms, makes anything other than a multi-activity, short unit, technique-focused approach extremely challenging. In Chapter 4 we will

6 *What Is Models-based Practice?*

return to what you as teachers might do about these curriculum and classroom arrangements to make MbP feasible.

For the public health, risk-management justification, the logic is compelling enough. If cardiovascular disease and obesity are the problems some authorities claim (though there have been dissenting voices from scholars like Michael Gard, 2010 about their rising prevalence), then a focus on MVPA seems desirable. The issue is, when priority is given to physical activity that makes students sweaty and huff and puff, what happens to learning? Learning appears to be displaced by the imperative to keep students physically active. It is possible that students may be learning about exercise as they engage in MVPA-focused physical education. But this seems a very limited aspiration.

Furthermore, as has also been pointed out, what if cardiovascular disease and obesity are not the only pressing health concerns facing society? What if, as the evidence from research is showing clearly, there is a rising prevalence of mental health issues among children and young people? How might this risk-management, MVPA, form of physical education help with this emerging crisis?

Why Models-based Practice?

It is within the context of what we see as serious limitations of the traditional dominant approach to physical education in practice that we consider arguments in favour of MbP. At the same time, we do not claim that MbP is, on the one hand, a cure for all of the ills within traditional physical education. Nor, on the other hand, is it the only possible alternative to the currently dominant approach. That said, we think there are at least three compelling reasons for giving MbP serious consideration.

First, MbP shifts what Metzler calls the 'organising centre' of physical education away from the currently dominant focus on content to the relationships among teaching, learning, curriculum (content) and assessment, that is, to pedagogy. Some national education systems, like England for example, are quite explicit about the use of big categories of content to organise physical education, such as games, athletics, dance, aquatics, gymnastics, and outdoor and adventurous activities. Others, like Scotland, use the concepts 'experiences and outcomes' and 'benchmarks' as their organisers, under the headings of physical competencies, cognitive skills, personal qualities and physical fitness. Even within this conceptual scheme, however, it is the major categories of content that are pencilled into practical units of work on the timetables of many schools.

In the case of the National Curriculum for Physical Education (NCPE) in England, the connection between what students should be taught to do and content is made explicit, even though the content is not legally required of schools. Similar connections are made in the case of the Curriculum for Excellence (CfE) in Scotland, as examples. But even with a conceptual framework to guide teachers in the Scottish case, the mention of content categories or indeed specific games and sports in our view reinforces the traditional approach of planning by content.

Pedagogical models also use content; how could they not? But they move away from content as the main organising principle of physical education and put it into a different relationship with the other elements of pedagogy. Indeed, as we will explain later, it is student learning that is the leading concern in pedagogical models, and teaching, curriculum and assessment are then brought into explicit alignment to realise the aspirations for student learning.

It is, then, the model that becomes the organising centre for MbP in physical education where the relationships among the elements of pedagogy are the explicit concerns in planning.

Second, and consequently, MbP offers a strong focus on student learning. Unlike the traditional, multi-activity approach, aspirations for student learning are specific and often unique to particular pedagogical models. For instance, in sport education, the learning aspirations for physically competent, literate and enthusiastic players, taken together, make the model distinctive. The development of the thinking player, tactical awareness and decision-making are key features of teaching games for understanding. These distinctive features of particular pedagogical models offer opportunities for you as a teacher to be much more focused on what you want your students to learn compared to traditional approaches.

Third, when you use two or more pedagogical models to organise physical education in your school or local collective of schools, and thus engage in MbP, you can select models that give your program a distinctive flavour. These models can be tailored to more precisely fit your situation, including the needs of your students. The main focus of particular models, which we call the 'main idea,' provides a good sense of how you might build this customised focus. For example, the main idea for sport education is to 'develop players in the fullest and richest sense.' For teaching games for understanding, it is 'fostering thinking players.' For cooperative learning, it is 'learning with, by, from and for each other.' For HbPE, it is 'valuing the physically active life.' For teaching personal and social responsibility, it is 'learning life skills concerned with personal and social responsibility.' There are other models which we will discuss in Chapter 3 that offer different and distinctive foci for program planning.

Of course, your selection and deployment of a range of pedagogical models over a school year must align with any national or district curricula that mandate the nature of school physical education. We believe it is possible to accommodate MbP within most national and district curricula. We will also address there how the selection and deployment of pedagogical models can be informed by your vision of your students' development over time and thus how you might sequence various pedagogical models within MbP.

What is a pedagogical model?

A pedagogical model is a mechanism through which to support teachers to design and implement the physical education programs in their schools.

In contrast to this idea, a common misunderstanding is that pedagogical models such as teaching games for understanding and sport education are actual physical education programs. If this is the case, they would need to provide much more detailed information in the form of lesson plans, learning tasks, assessment tasks and so on. Metzler (2011) does just this in his book on *Model-Based Instruction*. Nevertheless, he also sees (what he calls) instructional models in the same way as we view pedagogical models, as ways of supporting teachers to develop their own local programs.

This relationship between pedagogical models and local physical education programs is nowhere better illustrated than in the diagram we reproduced in the companion to this book from the work of Jewett and Bain (Casey & Kirk, 2021, p. 29). While Jewett and Bain use the terminology of 'curriculum model,' it is

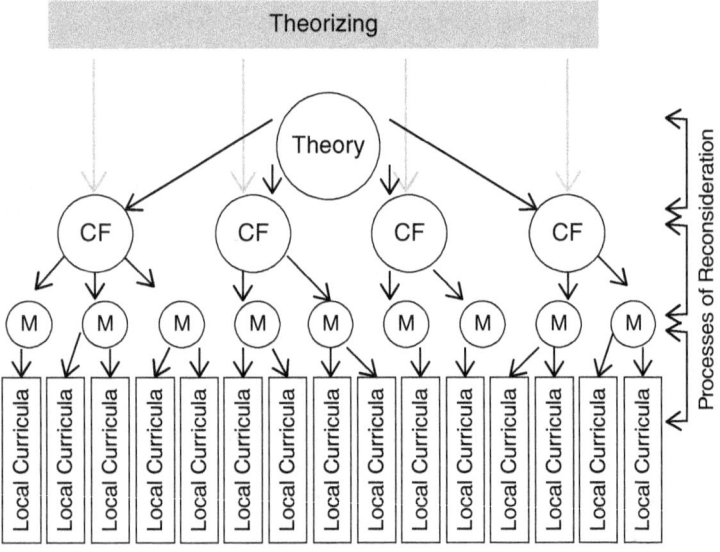

Key: CF = Conceptual Framework, M= Model

Figure 1.1 The process of model development (Casey & Kirk, 2021, p. 29) (Jewett & Bain, 1995) [Processes of reconsideration added by Casey (2016, p. 59)]

What Is Models-based Practice? 9

clear that they view models in precisely the same way as we do within MbP. In the diagram (see Figure 1.1 above), models are developed from curriculum theories and inform the design and development of 'local curricula.'

In case Jewett and Bain's scheme sounds somewhat top-down and linear, we added a feedback loop to the diagram which we call a process of reconsideration. This is essential in our view for the further and future development of pedagogical models, in the medium to longer term. The feedback loop allows teachers to test pedagogical models in practice and, over time, to suggest adaptations.

This notion, of testing models in practice, is consistent with Lawrence Stenhouse's (1975) formulation of the curriculum as a *specification*, rather than a *prescription*, for practice. Stenhouse's work supports our idea, introduced in this chapter, that pedagogical models are *design specifications*. They provide structure and guidance for program development at local levels. As a specification for practice, a pedagogical model is always to be viewed as provisional, in the sense that regular and ongoing adaptation of plans and programs will be necessary at the local level to meet new contingencies and sets of circumstances. For example, a new cohort of children in a class brings new capabilities and interests, new personalities and new classroom dynamics. If physical education is to be inclusive, fair and equitable, it is unlikely that last year's program will be suitable for this year's cohort, at least not in its entirety.

The structure of pedagogical models: practice architectures

There are a number of structural characteristics to all pedagogical models. We already mentioned that models are *pedagogical* because they include the four elements of teaching, learning, curriculum and assessment. These elements, we noted, are interrelated and interdependent. Because of this feature, pedagogical models cannot be reduced to any one of the elements.

This is a core idea about pedagogical models and what makes them organising centres for designing and developing physical education programs in schools. We are critical of the point that in traditional, multi-activity, sport technique-based forms of physical education, curriculum content by itself is typically the main organiser. Within pedagogical models, it is the relations among the four elements of pedagogy that become the organising centre of physical education programs.

The four elements are organised in a particular way. Learning outcomes or aspirations are highlighted as a leading concern in program design. The key question is, what do I want my students to learn? Once the learning outcomes or aspirations are identified, the next task is to align teaching, curriculum and assessment tightly in order to optimise the realisation of learning.

10 What Is Models-based Practice?

> We use both terms: 'learning outcomes' and 'aspirations.' In some pedagogical models it may be possible to specify in fairly precise terms the learning you want your students to demonstrate. 'Outcomes' would be the more suitable term to use in these circumstances. However, we recognise that it is not always possible to be precise with statements about learning, for example, within the affective domain. In such cases, when the learning is centred on motivation, resilience, perseverance, enjoyment and so on, aspirations may provide degrees of flexibility appropriate to these important but less tangible or concrete forms of learning.

This requirement for alignment assists you to consider the best content, teaching styles and assessment tasks that will most likely facilitate the learning you want for your students. Arguably, this is one of the significant weaknesses of traditional approaches to physical education, that is, a lack of tight alignment between the four elements of pedagogy. Pedagogical alignment is then one way in which pedagogical models offer an improvement for program design and development.

A second structural dimension of pedagogical models is that they all state a main idea, critical elements, and learning outcomes and aspirations. It is the substance of these three features of this structural dimension that permits each pedagogical model to make a distinctive and unique contribution to physical education programs.

We have already given some examples above of the main ideas of several well-known pedagogical models. If you recall, the main idea for sport education is to 'develop players in the fullest and richest sense,' while the main idea for teaching games for understanding is 'fostering thinking players.'

The critical elements build on the main idea. In sport education, the critical elements are seasons, affiliation, formal competition, culminating events, record-keeping and festivity. When designing and developing a program in your school based on the sport education pedagogical model, each of the critical elements will ideally be present in some form. The precise form the critical elements take will, however, differ from teacher to teacher and school to school. We think it is important that there is good (rather than complete) fidelity between the critical elements of a pedagogical model and the school program. This is because, arguably, where fidelity is strong, the learning outcomes or aspirations are more likely to be realised. When we talk about fidelity, however, we do not mean fidelity to procedure (i.e., copying a model from a textbook) but, instead, use McNeill et al.'s (2018) notion of fidelity to goals. After studying fidelity within the context of science education, these scholar teachers might do something that is different from the textbook but that is still consistent with the overarching goal of the intervention.

In conversations with teachers, we have sometimes talked about the critical elements of pedagogical models as the 'non-negotiable' features. Some scholars have misunderstood us on this point and argued that we are effectively prescribing what teachers must do. We disagree. When we have used the word 'non-negotiable,' what we mean is that the critical elements must be present in your school sport education program *in some form*, but that these elements may vary from class to class and between different schools. That said, different contexts determine what is possible (Curtner-Smith et al., 2021) and you shouldn't be concerned if you can't include every critical element as you begin to use a pedagogical model. Instead, this should be your aspiration as you become increasingly familiar with each different model.

Putting this slightly differently, if you want to claim you are doing 'sport education,' then we think it is reasonable to expect to see evidence of these critical elements. They are what makes sport education, sport education. The *in some form* caveat is important. This means one school may decide that, in addition to the common feature of creating teams as 'persisting groups,' affiliation can be promoted by encouraging students to make up a team name, or to devise a team chant, or to make a uniform by painting on a blank T-shirt, or indeed perhaps all or none of the above. There are many ways in which affiliation can be realised in sport education. How you go about this is down to your judgement, so long as affiliation is one of the features of the sport education program in your school.

Learning outcomes and aspirations again provide each pedagogical model with its distinctiveness. In sport education, it is the combination of the broad aspirations of enthusiastic, competent and literate sports people that gives this model its distinctive flavour. For teaching games for understanding, it is the combination of, for example, tactical decision-making, understanding how rules shape what's possible in terms of gameplay, recognising cues for action and appropriate skill performance that differentiates this model from others.

Practice architecture: sayings, doings, relatings

Together, these structural dimensions of all pedagogical models provide them with their 'practice architecture' (Kemmis & Grootenboer, 2008). The practice architecture of educational activities, particularly those within schools, comprise the specialised language and terminology used to talk about the activity (sayings), the specific practices themselves that teachers and students engage in (doings), and the relationships among teachers and students and students and students (relatings).

Within the pedagogy of each model, and their main ideas, critical elements and learning aspirations, there will be specific sayings, doings and relatings that distinguish one model from another.

An informed eavesdropper on a conversation between a physical education teacher and their students should be able to tell, by the language used, whether they were discussing, for example, sport education or teaching for personal and social responsibility (sayings).

An informed observer would be able to tell whether the practices they could see in the games hall or playing field were, for example, cooperative learning or teaching games for understanding (doings).

More difficult, perhaps, for the eavesdropper and observer to tell from relationships alone which model might be underway in a physical education lesson since there may be more commonality among models here than in sayings and doings. Just the same, it should be possible to tell from listening and observing whether the teacher respects and values the contribution of students individually and collectively. Furthermore, they should be able to discern whether students are able to work together constructively. Both aspects are key features of student-centred teaching (relatings).

Of course, it is the combinations of sayings, doings and relatings as expressions of pedagogy and of the main idea, critical elements and learning outcomes and aspirations that provide each pedagogical model with its distinctive and unique contribution to school physical education programs.

Conclusion

We argued in this chapter that Models-based Practice (MbP) has the potential to transform physical education in your school and challenge the conventional approaches that may have ensued. It does this by reorienting the subject's focal point away from sport-specific content towards pedagogy and student learning. Within MbP, pedagogy is positioned as the dynamic interplay of teaching, learning, curriculum and assessment. This quartet forms the fundamental basis for both pedagogical models and MbP itself.

MbP centres on practice (thus the P) and emphasises student-centric and developmentally appropriate approaches to physical education. This focus on practice is underscored by practice being model-based (i.e., Mb). By positioning pedagogical models as the organising centre of physical education, MbP empowers you, as teachers, to adopt diverse approaches while steering the subject away from traditional ideas and towards broader concepts of success in multiple domains of learning. A couple of compelling benefits arise from using MbP, notably its shift of focus from content to pedagogy, and its emphasis on student learning within the unique aspirations of each pedagogical model. Additionally, MbP helps you to create a tailored program through the inclusion of multiple pedagogical models in your program.

The chapter stresses that pedagogical models should be viewed as design specifications supporting teachers rather than blueprints. These models offer structure and guidance for local program development. Described as practice architectures, the structure of pedagogical models encompasses pedagogical alignment, a distinctive main idea, critical elements and learning aspirations/outcomes. It also includes the specialised language, specific practices and relationships defining each model. In essence, MbP emerges as a promising alternative to traditional physical education, highlighting the centrality of pedagogy and providing a comprehensive framework for the development of customised, student-focused programs.

References

Casey, A., & Kirk, D. (2021). *Models-based practice in physical education*. Routledge.

Casey, A. (2016). Models-based Practice. In C. D. Ennis (ed). *Routledge Handbook of Physical Education Pedagogies* (pp. 54–67). London: Routledge.

Casey, A., MacPhail, A., Larsson, H., & Quennerstedt, M. (2021). Between hope and happening: Problematizing the M and the P in models-based practice. *Physical Education and Sport Pedagogy*, *26*(2), 111–122.

Curtner-Smith, M. D., Kinchin, G. D., Hastie, P. A., Brunsdon, J. J., & Sinelnikov, O. A. (2021). "It's a lot less hassle and a lot more fun": Factors that sustain teachers' enthusiasm for and ability to deliver sport education. *Journal of Teaching in Physical Education*, *40*(2), 312–321.

Dyson, B., Howley, D., & Wright, P. M. (2021). A scoping review critically examining research connecting social and emotional learning with three model-based practices in physical education: Have we been doing this all along? *European Physical Education Review*, *27*(1), 76–95. https://doi.org/10.1177/1356336X20923710

Dyson, B., Kulinna, P., & Metzler, M. (2016). Introduction to the special issue: Models-based practice in physical education. *Journal of Teaching in Physical Education*, *35*, 297–298.

Gard, M. (2010). *The end of the obesity epidemic*. Routledge.

Jewett, A. E., & Bain, L. L. (1985). *The curriculum process in physical education*. Dubuque, IA: Wm. C. Brown.

Kemmis, S., & Grootenboer, P. (2008). Situating praxis in practice: Practice architectures and the cultural, social and material conditions for practice. In S. Kemmis & T. J. Smith (Eds.), *Enabling praxis: Challenges for education* (pp. 37–62). Sense.

Lund, J., & Tannehill, D (2014). *Standards-based Physical Education Curriculum Development* (3rd Edition). Burlington: Jones & Bartlett.

McKenzie, T. L., & Lounsbery, M. A. (2009). School physical education: The pill not taken. *American Journal of Lifestyle Medicine*, *3*(3), 219–225.

McNeill, K. L., Marco-Bujosa, L. M., González-Howard, M., & Loper, S. (2018). Teachers' enactments of curriculum: Fidelity to procedure versus fidelity to goal for scientific argumentation. *International Journal of Science Education*, *40*(12), 1455–1475.

Metzler, M. W. (2000). *Instructional models for physical education*. Holcomb Hathaway.

Metzler, M. W. (2011). *Instructional models for physical education* (3rd ed.). Holcomb Hathaway Publishers, Inc.

Metzler, M. W. (2017). *Instructional models for physical education* (3rd ed.). Routledge.

Sallis, J. F., & McKenzie, T. L. (1991). Physical education's role in public health. *Research Quarterly for Exercise and Sport*, *62*(2), 124–137.

Stenhouse, L. (1975). *An introduction to curriculum research and development*. Heinemann.

2 What pedagogical models exist?

In Chapter 1 we positioned MbP as a potential future for physical education and argued for the pedagogical model, with its main idea, critical elements, learning outcomes or aspirations and its pedagogy, to be the organising centre for physical education programs. In this chapter we will explore the range of pedagogical models currently available to teachers. We do this by categorising pedagogical models as either established or newly emerging pedagogical models.

Established pedagogical models

Among the list of well-established models we might include teaching games for understanding, sport education, cooperative learning, and teaching personal and social responsibility. An important issue to note with these four models is that they were not considered to be pedagogical models by their originators. In this sense, they pre-date the notion of pedagogical models (Haerens et al., 2011), instructional models (Metzler, 2000) and curriculum models (Jewett & Bain, 1985).

You might ask then, "How they can be considered to be pedagogical models or, indeed, models of any sort?" We think it is possible to fit the characteristic structures of pedagogical models to each of these approaches to physical education. We have already shown that it is possible to identify the key pedagogical features of these four well-established models and their main ideas, critical elements and learning outcomes or aspiration (see Casey & Kirk, 2021).

In fact, in doing this, we have followed the examples set by Lund and Tannehill (2005) and Metzler (2011). Lund and Tannehill identify 'personal and social responsibility,' 'teaching games for understanding' and 'sport education' among another five *curriculum models*. Metzler includes 'cooperative learning,' 'sport education,' 'tactical games,' and 'teaching personal and social responsibility' among his *instructional models*. These well-established models are re-worked in each case to fit the conceptual designs of Lund and Tannehill's and Metzler's, respectively.

DOI: 10.4324/9780429347078-2

In the next four subsections, we provide some detail about the practice architecture (the meta-practices of design and curriculum development that shape ideas about what will be taught and learnt in the local context [Kemmis & Grootenboer, 2008]) of each of the established models. For the most part we do this by 'retrofitting' to be consistent with the structural dimensions that make up the practice architectures of pedagogical models.

Sport education

In our retrofit of the original sport education approach developed by Siedentop (1994), the main idea, as we noted earlier, could be to develop players in the fullest and richest sense (Casey & Kirk, 2021, p. 43). The key features of Siedentop's approach then become the critical elements, including roles, seasons, affiliation, formal competition, record-keeping, festivity and a culminating event.

Learning aspirations can be organised around Siedentop's three large categories of competent, literate and enthusiastic players. While competence to play a game or sport is important, we think this should be the least emphasised group of learning aspirations for sport education itself, since these can be developed in other ways, for example, through teaching games for understanding or through the recently proposed 'practising' model (Aggerholm et al., 2018). The literacy and enthusiasm categories of learning aspirations suggest an emphasis on learning within the affective domain, perhaps casting sport education primarily as a pedagogy of affect[1] (Kirk, 2020).

In terms of pedagogy, the teacher would take on the role of activator (Goodyear & Dudley, 2015). Teaching has been found most effective when students were very active and directly involved in their own learning (Hattie, 2009). To this end, a key issue in sport education is to facilitate students being active in their own learning. Consequently, the teacher teaches values and respects the roles young people undertake. They would therefore resist the need to stop the whole class unless issues of safety were evident and direct their comments through the role holders. They would enable students by developing a classroom environment that allowed for festivity and celebration and which assessed competency, literacy and enthusiasm rather than skills and techniques.

Teaching games in physical education

There are various ways in which the main idea for a pedagogical model for teaching games in physical education can be expressed (Casey & Kirk, 2021, p. 47). Since one of us (Kirk, 2017) has already begun to work on the development of a new pedagogical model for teaching games (rather than retrofitting teaching games for understanding), we propose here a main idea of 'fostering thinking players.'

16 *What Pedagogical Models Exist?*

The critical elements of the retrofitted teaching games for understanding model would be each of the six elements of the Bunker-Thorpe approach (Casey & Kirk, 2021, p. 47). In our proposed new model, we have identified three critical elements: student-centredness, modified games and the setting of problems to be solved by the players.

As our retrofit of the teaching games for understanding approach shows, we could set a wide range of learning aspirations. For the new pedagogical model, we opt to list key learning aspirations in three nested categories of individual, small group and whole (modified) game.

In terms of pedagogy, with learning aspirations identified in each of these interdependent categories, alignment with teaching, curriculum (content) and assessment should be tight. Since student-centredness is a critical element, teaching is most likely to be facilitative, such as guided discovery (in Mosston and Ashworth's (2002) terms), with question and answer a central feature of the relationships between teacher and students (Butler, 1997) and also among students themselves through, for example, the 'debate of ideas' (Grehaigne et al., 2005). Content will comprise both individual and team games, mostly in the form of games modified to match the learners' current readiness to learn. Assessment needs to be clearly aligned with individual, group and whole game contexts and needs to consider the 'thinking player,' that is, their decision-making as well as their skill execution. Reflecting on the critical elements of setting problems to be solved, assessment might focus on the performance of tasks judged against appropriate criteria at individual, group and whole group levels (Barquero-Ruiz et al., 2021; QCAA, 2019).

Cooperative learning

A main idea of a retrofitted cooperative learning model could be learning with, by, from and for each other. Drawing on the work of Johnson and Johnson (1991), Dyson and Casey (2016) argued for at least five critical elements: promotive face-to-face interaction, positive interdependence, individual accountability, small group and interpersonal skills, and group processing.

Dyson and Casey (2016) also list a number of learning aspirations for students reflecting the emphasis on group work and interpersonal skills. This is another model that might be viewed as a pedagogy of affect, featuring togetherness, responsibility to self and others, communication skills and feeling safe.

In terms of pedagogy, the teacher would put cooperation, and its facets of social interdependence, accountability, group over individual decisions and teamwork, ahead of skill development. Content would be devised to maximise student interactions, and groups would be kept small enough to ensure that voice and choice were present. Finally, assessment would need to consider cooperation rather than competence, with students being able to put the needs of the many ahead of the needs of the few or the one (Casey & Fernandez-Rio, 2019).

Teaching personal and social responsibility

Casey and Kirk (2021, p. 58) suggest a main idea in teaching personal and social responsibility of learning life skills concerned with personal and social responsibility. In contrast, Hellison (1995, the originator of this approach) may have insisted on adding the life skills of alienated youth, since these were the young people he worked with. Over many years of this work, Hellison established a number of key activities that we might recast in a retrofitted pedagogical model as critical elements, such as activities aimed at facilitating self and collective awareness, five levels of responsibility in action, times for reflection and decision-making about responsibility, and activities that develop respect, care and trust.

While a range of specific learning aspirations might arise from the main idea and critical elements, Hellison's (1995) five cumulative levels of responsibility provide a concrete and workable process for teachers. Level zero, for Hellison, was little or no responsibility, which we cannot propose as a learning aspiration, but as something to move on from. At level one, respect, students can control their behaviour and not disrupt others' learning, working under the close supervision of the teacher. Level two, participation, sees a student participating willingly but still under the teacher's supervision. At level three, students are able to self-direct their own activity. Level four, caring, shows students able to work with, support and assist others to learn. Hellison suggested one further level: that these life skills are transferable from the gym to wider, everyday life. Once again, with this focus for learning, we could identify TPSR model as a pedagogy of affect (Kirk, 2020).

In terms of pedagogy, given the learning aspirations for this model, teaching will generally be facilitative in style. This said, we note the requirement for levels one and two of teacher supervision, so there may be also a need for some teacher direction. Indeed, TPSR moves the teacher from direction to facilitation/activation across the levels. Curriculum content tends to be strongly influenced by student choice and can be either group or individual activities. While the learning aspirations of this model are firmly in the affective domain, Hellison stressed the importance to students that they were practising to become better at the chosen activity, since this he saw as a key to motivating them. Hellison (1995, pp. 69–70) used a range of assessment strategies to monitor student progress, including simple self-evaluation questionnaires, tracking relevant student behaviour, keeping a teacher journal and talking regularly with other adults about student learning progression.

18 *What Pedagogical Models Exist?*

Summary

As can be seen from the above, our first category of pedagogical models consists of a number of well-known and established approaches to physical education that can be successfully 'retrofitted' to the structures we set out in the first chapter. These four models, unsurprisingly, have also been widely studied in practice, though not necessarily in their form as pedagogical models. There is, nevertheless, a strong body of empirical data available not only about their effectiveness but also about teachers' and students' positive experiences of using them.

> There have been several systematic reviews of different pedagogical models, and for a better understanding of the empirical data available, we would recommend you read:
> Baptista et al. (2020) and/or Richards and Shriver (2020) – teaching personal and social responsibility
> Casey and Goodyear (2015) – cooperative learning
> Harvey and Jarrett (2014) – game-centred approaches
> Hastie et al. (2011) and/or Hastie and Wallhead (2016) – sport education
> The importance of these reviews of empirical studies of these models is that each has been tested in practice and, by and large, found to be successful in providing their intended educational benefits.

Next, we consider a number of newly emerging pedagogical models.

Emerging pedagogical models

There is a second category of pedagogical models which we will describe here as emerging. These are approaches where physical education scholars have sought to use the structural dimensions we have outlined previously as starting points for the design and development of new pedagogical models. We describe five emerging pedagogical models at various stages of development. We do this in an effort to open your eyes to a wider scope of pedagogical models, but this is not an exhaustive list. Our hope is that as your school program develops towards MbP, you will find more models through which to develop the young people in your care.

Activist pedagogical model for working with girls

The activist pedagogical model has developed out of two decades of Kim Oliver's activist work with adolescent and younger girls. In a 2015 publication, Oliver and Kirk joined forces to use Kim's carefully researched and developed approach and David's knowledge of MbP to construct a pedagogical model. The main idea for this model is girls learning to value the physically active life. Four enduring features emerged from Oliver's research to form the critical elements of student-centredness, pedagogies of embodiment, inquiry-based education centred-*in*-action and listening to respond over time.

The learning aspirations for the activist model are girls learning to name, critique, negotiate and, where possible, change barriers to their participation in physical activity. Casey and Kirk (2021, p. 60) identify a number of other more specific learning aspirations out of these four, relating to critical literacy skills, perseverance and resilience, and the co-construction by students and teachers of physical education programs.

In terms of pedagogy, teaching within this model is generally facilitative, given the focus on student-centredness and co-construction of programs. Selection of curriculum content is done by students guided by the teacher. In the first phase of this activist model, 'Building the Foundation,' following several sessions in which students and the teacher work together to learn more about their needs and interests, students are able to sample a range of physical activities that are unfamiliar to them. This sampling then informs the selection of activities during the second phase, where content is organised thematically. Assessment for this model could resemble the various research techniques Oliver has used over time to investigate girls' responses to activist pedagogy, including structured in-class discussions, visual methods such as drawing and photography, and the production by students of artefacts such as a book of games that girls can play.

The resultant pedagogical model developed from Oliver and Kirk's collaboration has been tested in practice with five teachers in Scottish secondary schools, showing that teachers were able to learn to use the model and apply it in their own settings to develop co-constructed programs with their students (Oliver et al., 2018; Kirk et al., 2018; Lamb et al., 2018). Other research has been undertaken using Oliver's activist approach (e.g., Enright & O'Sullivan, 2012; Fisette, 2013; Walseth et al., 2018), though not specifically using the pedagogical model. The model has since been strengthened and clarified through its location with a salutogenic theory of health promotion (Kirk, 2020). This theory provides a strengths-based approach to curriculum development, which involves the identification and employment of assets for health promotion (McCuaig et al., 2013).

Socially vulnerable youth pedagogical model

The socially vulnerable youth pedagogical model grew directly out of Oliver's activist work with girls (Luguetti et al., 2017). In this case, however, the focus was on young people living in the favelas[2] of Santos, a large city in Brazil, and the site for the development of the model was a community soccer and judo club catering mainly, though not exclusively, for boys. Social vulnerability in this context referred to exposure to and first-hand experience of drug trafficking, alcohol and substance abuse, organised crime, domestic violence, violence on the streets and grinding poverty.

The main idea of the model was co-constructing empowering possibilities through sport for these young people. Two critical elements from the activist pedagogical model were drawn into this model: student-centredness and inquiry-based education centred-*in*-action. Another three were added: an ethic of care, a community of sport and attentiveness to community. Four aspirations for learning emerged for this model. These were becoming responsible and committed, communicating with others, valuing each other's knowledge and learning from mistakes.

In terms of pedagogy and given these learning aspirations, the teaching and curriculum content were intertwined. Ostensibly, the youth were participating in the two activities the club offered: soccer and judo. However, the physical activities themselves were a vehicle for the teaching of other things such as responsibility, commitment, communication and caring. This is not to say that the physical activity vehicles were unimportant but development in those were deemed less important than development in the specific learning aspirations. As is also the case with an activist model and teaching personal and social responsibility, the physical activities are excellent media for the development of life skills. Assessment in the context of the social vulnerability model rested in this developmental work on the extent to which the youth persisted in their participation at the club, whether they went to school regularly and whether they stayed out of trouble with gangs.

Health-based physical education pedagogical model

The idea of the health-based physical education (HbPE) pedagogical model was first sketched out and proposed by Haerens et al. (2011) but owes its existence to the doctoral work of Mark Bowler and Paul Sammon at Loughborough University (see Bowler et al., 2022). Working with two secondary schools and numerous cohorts of pre-service teachers, Bowler and Sammon developed a conceptual framework for HbPE and then trialled the model in schools before entering into the process of reconceptualisation we talked about earlier in the book.

HbPE was developed in reaction to the enduring critique that physical education programs too frequently place their emphasis on fitness, exercise and health and to counter the mismatch between teachers' well-meaning philosophies (usually a 'fitness for life' goal or similar) and their practice (which tends to focus on 'fitness for sport/performance' [Harris & Leggett, 2015]).

The main idea of HbPE is "Valuing a physically active life," which could be simplified to valuing movement. Valuing movement is closely aligned with the notions of meaningfulness and intrinsic motivation, which are fundamental characteristics that support a commitment to physical activity participation (Fletcher et al., 2021). The critical elements of HbPE are teacher *promotes* meaningful

What Pedagogical Models Exist? 21

physical activity, teacher supports students to be *informed* movers; teacher creates a *needs-supportive* learning environment; and teacher encourages students to become *critical* movers. To help practitioners remember the critical elements, Bowler and Sammon created the acronym PINC, that is, promotes, informed, needs-supportive, critical movers. Four learning aspirations in HbPE are habitual movers (engage in regular movement), motivated movers (value movement), informed movers (know how, when and where to be active) and critical movers (promote physical activity locally among friends, family and community).

In terms of pedagogy, HbPE identifies five assumptions of learning and teaching to guide teachers in their design and implementation of the model: (1) teachers prioritise a physical activity for life (rather than a fitness, sport or performance) approach, (2) changes in physical activity behaviour require extended periods of learning, (3) what is learnt in HbPE must be meaningful and draw from and be transferable into young people's leisure time, (4) approaches must develop students' intrinsic motivation for physical activity and (5) HbPE programs should draw on multiple school, family and community strategies.

Practising pedagogical model

The practising pedagogical model was theorised and developed in Scandinavia by Aggerholm, Standal, Barker and Larsson in recognition that practising was not well represented in physical education. Building on the work of Arendt (1958) and Sloterdijk (2012), Aggerholm et al. (2018) argued that while physical education is dominated by health and exercise and sport and games, it fails to adequately consider the student's experiences of, and learning from, practising particular skills or competencies.

Centred on the notion that practising refers to the ways in which actions occur rather than the actions themselves, the main idea of the practising model is an acceptance of better and worse ways of practising. Seven critical elements are central to this model: agency, content, goal, verticality, effort, uncertainty and repetition. The four learning outcomes are: acknowledging subjectivity and providing meaningful challenges, focusing on content and the aims of practising, specifying and negotiating strands of excellence, and providing adequate time for practising.

In terms of pedagogy and given these learning outcomes, the aim for teachers is to stimulate and facilitate practising and find ways to help students find an interest in practising. This would be done without giving specific instructions or explanations. Instead, teachers provide meaningful and well-adapted challenges that help students, on an individual level, work in the space between 'I can' and 'I cannot.' Teachers also help each student to constitute their own understanding of what excellence means to them. From an assessment perspective, more emphasis is placed on supporting students' process of practising rather than on the summative assessment of learning.

Spectrum of teaching styles

Positioning the spectrum in this book wasn't an easy decision given that Muska Mosston's original book was published in 1966. That said, the two recent works by SueSee, Pill, Davies and Williams are the only ones positioning the spectrum as a pedagogical model. Given that these were published in 2022 and 2023, respectively, we've taken the decision to explore the spectrum in the emerging pedagogical models section of this chapter while acknowledging that this work has existed in physical education for the better part of 60 years.

The spectrum of teaching styles was originally published in 1966 and is currently in its sixth edition (Mosston & Ashworth, 2008). In considering it as a pedagogical model, however, the writing of Pill, SueSee, Davies and Williams gives the clearest insight into its inclusion in the MbP literature. Pill et al. (2023) argue that some models, like sport education and game-based approaches, refer to what to teach (e.g., competence, literacy, and enthusiasm or roles other than performer in the case of sport education). In contrast, other models, like cooperative learning, don't seek to define content and are, instead, ways of structuring the 'how' of teaching rather than the 'what' of teaching. If we take this argument further and compare the 11 non-versus Landmark styles (Mosston & Ashworth, 2008; Pill et al., 2023; SueSee et al., 2021) with the "set of principles and methods" (Slavin, 1990, p. xi) inherent in cooperative learning, such as its structural approach (Kagan, 1993) or its curricular approach (Slavin, 1999), then it is easier to see how the spectrum mirrors other pedagogical models in its flexibility and adaptability. As such, any of the 11 styles (Command, style-A; practice, style-B; reciprocal, style-C; self-check, style-D; inclusion, style-E; guided discovery, style-F; convergent discovery, style-G; divergent discovery, style-H; learner designed I.P., style-I; learner initiated, style-J; self-teaching, style-K), or indeed a number of them, could be used in any given lesson or unit of work.

In asserting "the Spectrum's legitimacy in MBP" Pill et al. (2023, p. 2) present the spectrum as a pedagogical model "due to its 'organising centre' that pedagogical decisions and landmark teaching styles are determined in a chain of decision-making between the teacher and learner." They hold that the spectrum doesn't define content, nor does it control what should be taught; this is the role of national and state curricula. Instead, the spectrum seeks to develop the "cognitive capacities [of] learners . . . for reproductive thinking and productive thinking" (SueSee et al., 2022, p. 642). Consequently, any of the 11 styles (some of which sit under the reproductive banner [styles A to E] and some of the productive banners [styles F to K]) are valued in terms of student learning (as structures are valued in cooperative learning or pedagogies of embodiment are valued in the activist approach).

In preparing to write this sub-section, we reached out to Brendan SueSee and Shane Pill and asked them to help us articulate the spectrum using the four elements of a pedagogical model that we proposed in our last book (Casey & Kirk, 2021). We did this both due to our unfamiliarity with the spectrum as a pedagogical model and our familiarity with the spectrum as a widely used approach in physical education. We believe that what they sent stands a fitting conclusion to this section and will help you to position the spectrum in any MbP approach you take in your school.

> **Main Idea**
>
> One teaching style cannot accomplish education in all domains of learning (cognitive, physical, social, emotional, ethical) due to student diversity and the needs of multi-dimensional curriculum documents. No style is wrong, but a style can be wrongly applied – this is known as a non-versus approach. The intention is mobility ability within the Spectrum, as teaching is a chain of deliberate decision-making between the teacher and students. Understanding the who, what and when of the decision-making leads to the teaching style chosen to meet the learning objective.
>
> **Critical Elements**
>
> Alignment between the choice of teaching styles (and the creation of episodes using styles A–K), the chosen learning objectives (physical, social, emotional, cognitive and ethical) and the cognitive operation stated in the objective – namely, recalling skills/knowledge/tactics, discovering answers to unknown problems or creating two or more solutions to unknown problems.
>
> **Learning Aspirations**
>
> A student taught through the 11 styles experiences a wide range of decisions in their learning and ultimately has the potential to become 'free' from the teacher being the only person who sets the objectives, teaching behaviour, learning style and learner behaviour during their learning.
>
> **Pedagogy**
>
> Every teaching episode is a chain of decision-making from the pre-impact (planning), impact (delivery) and post-impacts (reflection) activities. The teaching style (A-K) is chosen to meet these specific objectives.
>   SueSee and Pill (personal communication, December 20, 2023)

Conclusion

The aim of this chapter was to explore a range of pedagogical models currently available to teachers. We did this by categorising pedagogical models as either well-established or newly emerging models. What is common across the nine models we explored (and others we did not) is the aspiration to organise physical education in schools around different main ideas, critical elements, learning aspirations and pedagogies rather than on the singular focus on sport techniques and traditional games taught through a single 'one-size-fits-all' approach, both of which have been extensively criticised in physical education.

MbP, and its component parts (i.e., pedagogical models), is not an approach that aspires to achieve one thing. It has varying intentions and is specific to local curricula. MbP is founded on the aspiration to achieve different outcomes and use different practices in its quest to achieve differing aims. The examples given here are not an exhaustive list. There are many other models but developing a program in your school that incorporates these eight models would allow teachers to create a physical education experience for their students that strives to do distinctive things in diverse ways. In the next chapter we will unpack different models and help you prepare to succeed with MbP.

Notes

1 An approach to education that places emphasis on emotions, feelings and affective experiences as central to learning and growth.
2 Informal settlement/shantytown.

References

Aggerholm, K., Standal, O., Barker, D. M., & Larsson, H. (2018). On practising in physical education: Outline for a pedagogical model. *Physical Education and Sport Pedagogy*, *23*(2), 197–208.

Arendt, H. (1958). *The human condition*. The University of Chicago Press.

Baptista, C., Corte-Real, N., Regueiras, L., Seo, G., Hemphill, M., Pereira, A., Dias, C., Martinek, T. and Fonseca, A. (2020). Teaching personal and social responsibility after school: A systematic review. *Cuadernos de Psicología del Deporte*, *20*(2), pp. 1–25.

Barquero-Ruiz, C., Kirk, D., & Arias-Estero, J. L. (2021). Design and validation of the tactical assessment instrument in football (TAIS). *Research Quarterly for Exercise and Sport*, *93*. https://doi.org/10.1080/02701367.2021.1889457

Bowler, M., Sammon, P., & Casey, A. (2022). Health-based physical education: A pedagogical model. In L. Cale & J. Harris (Eds.), *Physical education pedagogies for health* (pp. 62–76). Routledge.

Butler, J. (1997). How would Socrates teach games? A constructivist approach. *Journal of Physical Education, Recreation & Dance*, *68*(9), 42–47. https://doi.org/10.1080/07303084.1997.10605029

Casey, A., & Fernandez-Rio, J. (2019). Cooperative learning and the affective domain. *Journal of Physical Education, Recreation & Dance*, *90*(3), 12–17. https://doi.org/10.1080/07303084.2019.1559671

Casey, A., & Goodyear, V. A. (2015). Can cooperative learning achieve the four learning outcomes of physical education? A review of literature. *Quest*, *67*(1), 56–72.

Casey, A., & Kirk, D. (2021). *Models-based practice in physical education*. Routledge.

Dyson, B., & Casey, A. (2016). *Cooperative learning in physical education and physical activity: A practical introduction*. Routledge.
Enright, E., & O'Sullivan, M. (2012). Physical education "in all sorts of corners". *Research Quarterly for Exercise and Sport, 83*(2), 255–267.
Fisette, J. L. (2013). "Are you listening?" Adolescent girls voice how they negotiate self-identified barriers to their success and survival in physical education. *Physical Education and Sport Pedagogy, 18*(2), 184–203.
Fletcher, T., D. Ní Chróinín, D. Gleddie, and S. Beni(Eds.). 2021. *Meaningful Physical Education: An Approach for Teaching and Learning*. Abingdon: Routledge.
Goodyear, V. A., & Dudley, D. (2015). I'm a facilitator of learning! Understanding what teachers and students do within student-centered physical education models. *Quest, 67*(3), 274–289.
Grehaigne, J. F., Richard, J. F., & Griffin, L. L. (2005). *Teaching and learning team sports and games*. Routledge.
Haerens, L., Kirk, D., Cardon, G., & Bourdeauhuji, I. (2011) The development of a pedagogical model for Health-Based Physical Education, *Quest*, 63, 321–338.
Harris, J., & Leggett, G. (2015). Influences on the expression of health within PE curricula in secondary schools in England and Wales. *Sport, Education and Society, 20*(7), 908–923.
Harvey, S., & Jarrett, K. (2014). A review of the game-centred approaches to teaching and coaching literature since 2006. *Physical Education and Sport Pedagogy, 19*(3), 278–300.
Hastie, P. A., de Ojeda, D. M., & Calderón, A. (2011). A review of research on sport education: 2004 to the present. *Physical Education and Sport Pedagogy, 16*(2), 103–132.
Hastie, P. A., & Wallhead, T. (2016). Models-based practice in physical education: The case for sport education. *Journal of Teaching in Physical Education, 35*(4), 390–399.
Hattie, J. (2009). *Visible learning: A synthesis of over 800 meta-analyses relating to achievement*. Routledge.
Hellison, D. (1995). *Teaching responsibility through physical activity*. Human Kinetics.
Jewett, A. E., & Bain, L. L. (1985). *The curriculum process in physical education*. Wm. C. Brown.
Johnson, D. W., & Johnson, R. T. (1991). *Learning together and alone: Cooperative, competitive and individualistic learning* (3rd ed.). Prentice Hall.
Kagan, S. (1993). *Cooperative learning*. Kagan Cooperative Learning.
Kemmis, S., & Grootenboer, P. (2008). Situating praxis in practice: Practice architectures and the cultural, social and material conditions for practice. In S. Kemmis & T. J. Smith (Eds.), *Enabling praxis: Challenges for education* (pp. 37–62). Rotterdam: Sense.
Kirk, D. (2017). Teaching games in physical education: Towards a pedagogical model. *Revista Portuguesa de Ciencias do Desporto, 17*(S1.A), 17–26.
Kirk, D. (2020). *Precarity, critical pedagogy and physical education*. Routledge.
Kirk, D., Lamb, C. A., Oliver, K. L., Ewing-Day, R., Fleming, C., Loch, A., & Smedley, V. (2018). Balancing prescription with teacher and pupil agency: Spaces for manoeuvre within a pedagogical model for working with adolescent girls. *The Curriculum Journal, 29*(2), 219–237.
Lamb, C. A., Oliver, K. L., & Kirk, D. (2018). "Go for it girl" adolescent girls' responses to the implementation of an activist approach in a core

physical education programme. *Sport, Education and Society, 23*(8), 799–811.
Luguetti, C., Oliver, K. L., Kirk, D., & Dantas, L. (2017). Exploring an activist approach of working with boys from socially vulnerable backgrounds in a sport context. *Sport, Education and Society, 22*(4), 493–510.
Lund, J., & Tannehill, D. (2005). *Standards-based physical education curriculum development.* Jones & Bartlett Publishers.
McCuaig, L., Quennerstedt, M., & Macdonald, D. (2013). A salutogenic, strengths-based approach as a theory to guide HPE curriculum change. *Asia-Pacific Journal of Health, Sport and Physical Education, 4*(2), 109–125.
Metzler, M.W. (2000). *Instructional Models for Physical Education.* Needham Heights, Massachusetts: Allyn and Bacon.
Metzler, M. W. (2011). *Instructional models for physical education* (2nd ed.). Routledge.
Mosston, M. (1966). *Teaching physical education.* Merrill.
Mosston, M., & Ashworth, S. (2002). Teaching physical education (5th ed.). Boston, MA: Benjamin Cummings.
Mosston, M., & Ashworth, S. (2008). *Teaching physical education* (1st online ed.). Spectrum Institute for Teaching and Learning. https://spectrumofteachingstyles.org/assets/files/book/Teaching_Physical_Edu_1st_Online.pdf
Oliver, K. L., & Kirk, D. (2015). *Girls, gender and physical education: An activist approach.* Routledge.
Oliver, K. L., Luguetti, C., Aranda, R., Nuñez Enriquez, O., & Rodriguez, A.-A. (2018). "Where do I go from here?" Learning to become activist teachers through a community of practice. *Physical Education and Sport Pedagogy, 23*(2), 150–165.
Pill, S., SueSee, B., & Davies, M. (2023). The spectrum of teaching styles and models-based practice for physical education. *European Physical Education Review, 30.* https://doi.org/10.1177/1356336X231189146
QCAA (Queensland Curriculum and Assessment Authority). (2019). *Subject enrolments and levels of achievement – 2018.* www.qcaa.qld.edu.au/downloads/publications/qcaa_stats_sen_subjects_2018.pdf
Richards, K. A. R., & Shiver, V. N. (2020). "What's Worth Doing?": A Qualitative Historical Analysis of the TPSR Model. *Journal of Teaching in Physical Education, 39*(3), 300–310.
Siedentop, D. (1994). *Sport education: Quality PE through positive sport experiences.* Human Kinetics.
Slavin, R. E. (1990). *Cooperative learning: Theory, research and practice.* Allyn and Bacon.
Slavin, R. E. (1999). Comprehensive approaches to co-operative learning. *Theory into Practice, 38*(2), 74–79.
Sloterdijk, P. (2012). *The art of philosophy: Wisdom as a practice* (K. Margolis, Trans.). Columbia University Press.
SueSee, B., Pill, S., Davies, M., & Williams, J. (2021). "Getting the tip of the pen on the paper": How the spectrum of teaching styles narrows the gap between the hope and the happening. *Journal of Teaching in Physical Education, 41*(4), 640–649.
Walseth, K., Engebretsen, B., & Elvebakk, L. (2018). Meaningful experiences in PE for all students: An activist research approach. *Physical Education and Sport Pedagogy, 23*(3), 235–249.

3 Preparing to succeed with MbP

Playing the long game

> In embracing the new, the practitioner must make themselves comfortable with discomfort, and understand that confusion, uncertainty, and doubt are to be embraced.
>
> (Casey et al., 2017, p. 4)

The above quotation comes from a book on practitioner research but the same could be said about both the use of a pedagogical model and the decision to engage in MbP. Using a pedagogical model for the first time is not without its challenges nor is it unique with tens of thousands of teachers (including yourself perhaps) having already given it a go. Past experiences show, however, that, as with any skill worth learning, using pedagogical models and MbP effectively in your context, and to the best effect, takes time.

In his review of literature on MbP, Ash described five dominant themes in the collective research on pedagogical models:

(i) *change for teachers* (pedagogical models are something different and need to be prepared for and given time to embed in a school),

(ii) *difficulty and time* (embedding a model wasn't necessarily easy and took time to achieve),

(iii) *diversification in the teacher's role* (pedagogical models took the teacher away from the role of instructor and required them, instead, to activate or facilitate learning),

(iv) *evidence of effectiveness* (teachers often wanted to see evidence that any given pedagogical model worked before they were willing to give it a go), and

(v) *university/teacher collaboration* (the introduction of pedagogical models works best when teachers and researchers support each other).

Casey (2014, p. 23)

DOI: 10.4324/9780429347078-3

MbP is different from other forms of physical education. Your role as a teacher will be different, the role of the students will be different, and the organising centre is different. This amount of change takes both time and effort. Our advice is "be prepared to play the long game" from the start. This will take the pressure off and will allow everyone, even the biggest sceptics in your department or school, the opportunity to experience different models, hopefully change their minds and then adapt to the change that's coming. It will also give you the time, as we'll discuss in the next section, to lay the groundwork. Such preparation is important and will enable your aspirations for pedagogical change to prosper and flourish.

Be prepared to change the way you behave in your lessons. You are potentially moving from what Zhao (2020, p. 102) described as a "'do after me' paradigm, i.e., a teacher modelling and student-imitating configuration" to a series of different approaches that require you, the students, the subject matter, the curriculum and assessment to play different roles. If, for example, you are using an activist approach or teaching personal and social responsibility, then the students will have a say on the curriculum. In comparison, if you are using a cooperative learning approach, the subject matter will be secondary to your learning aspirations in the social and affective domains. Whichever way you develop your approach to MbP, it will probably be new and may well require you to be comfortable with discomfort.

The groundwork

In Chapter 4 we advocate for the need to work collectively and collaboratively with colleagues, students and other stakeholders, and in Chapter 5 we explore the need to make a case for MbP. In addition to these ideas are the need to (1) manage the timetable, (2) move away from a multi-activity, sport technique-based approach to physical education and (3) find help from others. All these things probably fit under the umbrella of groundwork. They are, however, less foundational than the ideas we present in this chapter, and as such we have taken the decision to discuss them later. Indeed, preparing the ground for MbP is different from preparing the ground to use one or two pedagogical models.

But why?

Because using one or two pedagogical models has been done by teachers many thousands (perhaps tens of thousands) of times. Furthermore, using one or two models in a multi-activity curriculum (with its short units of work) has been shown to be successful and is probably where you want to start. Not everything is straightforward though; there will be challenges and inevitably not everything will work. Pedagogical models are not all sunshine and lollypops. There will also be limits to what you can achieve with one model, which is why we advocate for a multi-model approach.

Most research exploring the use of different pedagogical models has investigated their use in multi-activity curricula, and this body of work might best be defined as a celebration of the potential of each pedagogical model. Thus, the first step in MbP is choosing your first model or models. It is as simple as rereading Chapter 2, deciding on the main idea, critical elements, learning outcomes or aspirations and pedagogy that best appeal to you and getting started. Find some books or practitioner articles – the Internet is replete with them – and learn about the basics of any given model. Maybe go back to your old university notes and see what came up before. Either way, learn what the expectations and aspirations of your chosen pedagogical models are and start to think about what you want to do (there is a more detailed consideration of this process in Chapter 4).

It is important to consider your teaching against the aspirations for the model. Fifteen years ago, Curtner-Smith et al. (2008) coined the terms 'full version,' 'watered-down version' and 'cafeteria approach' to describe student teachers' use of sport education. They argued that some student teachers chose, as you would in a cafeteria, specific aspects (e.g., roles and responsibilities) of a pedagogical model they liked (in this case sport education) but didn't go any further. Others used a watered-down approach when they chose to use some of what we now see as critical elements (i.e., formal competition, roles and enduring teams) but continued, for example, to teach the skills or referee/umpire the games that were played themselves. In some cases, student teachers "delivered full units, units that replicated the spirit of Siedentop's [the creator of sport education] intentions" (Curtner-Smith et al., 2008, p. 102).

In some respects, you need to decide the same. Which of these approaches (cafeteria, watered-down or full) are you going to use, and do you have the capacity to go further? Remember that local circumstances will play a role in what you are able to do. Remember also that these different versions might be viewed on a continuum (i.e., cafeteria approach, watered-down or full) and that, as a teacher, you might be on a journey towards enacting sport education. Careful consideration of how sport education might be used in response to different aspects of your school's culture will be important (Curtner-Smith et al., 2021). That said, also be aware that cafeteria and watered-down approaches to sport education are not the same as using a sport education approach. This only happens when the main idea, critical elements, learning outcome and aspirations, and pedagogy of sport education are actualised within your local context.

Learning to teach and learning to learn in new ways

One of the key things we learnt through Ash's research is that not only are you and your colleagues learning to teach in new ways but the students are also learning to learn in new ways. They are used to physical education being about multiple activities and skills and you want to change that. Therefore, we recommend taking things slowly. Do not try and do everything immediately but go through some 'basic training.'

So, you have chosen your first model or two (let's say that they're sport education and cooperative learning), and now you need to get a sense of each model's main idea, critical elements, learning outcomes/aspirations and pedagogy and decide how you are going to implement them in your school. Figure 3.1 breaks down a practice architecture (Kemmis & Grootenboer, 2008) (discussed later in the chapter) of a pedagogical model (exploring the main idea, critical elements, learning aspirations and pedagogy). It is important to note that the student is at the heart of this and that pedagogical choices around teaching, learning, curriculum and assessment are made with them in mind.

Figures 3.2. to 3.7 provide examples of what a practice architecture of the practising model, sport education, teaching games for understanding (TGfU), teaching personal and social responsibility (TPSR), the activist model, and health-based physical education might look like.

We assume that you are reading this book because you have already decided to or are trying to decide if you could and/or should change your physical education program. You might have come to this decision because you have doubts about your current provision:

- Is it fit for purpose?
- Do some things endure simply because that's the way you've always done them?
- Have your priorities for the young people in your care changed?
- Do you just want to do something different, and you want to give MbP a try?

Whatever the reason, you are at the first step of a staircase towards pedagogical change. Not everyone will walk the subsequent staircase in the same way. Some might fly up it three steps at a time, while others might take a more measured pace, one step at a time (and may revisit a step or two on their way). Some might have a look but may not like the view they get of physical education and return to what is familiar. The important thing to remember is you do not have to plan everything you want to undertake in order to take your first few steps.

You now need to choose what it is you want to change. Perhaps you want to help your students to work together with a shares purpose and in an environment where only working together will get results? Or perhaps you want to play developmentally appropriate games where students take on roles other than that of performer? In the first instance you might choose cooperative learning and in the later, sport education.

Let us say you want students to work together with a shared purpose, and you choose cooperative learning. Now you need to take the first step, bearing in mind, as we explain in detail in Chapters 4 and 5, that this is a shared and collective process with a range of stakeholders, colleagues and students included. You do not suddenly have to start with a whole grade; you might simply choose a class or two to try it out with. Alternatively, each member of your department might choose a different class and you might pool resources

A practice architecture of a pedagogical model

#1. Main Idea
The main purpose and character of a model.

#2. Critical Elements
Provide a pedagogical model with its distinctive 'shape' as well as giving users some sense of what the creators of the model regard as its unique and essential features.

#3. Learning Aspirations
Relate specifically to the main idea or theme of the model. Learning aspirations involve differentiation in learning tasks, teaching styles and assessment practices.

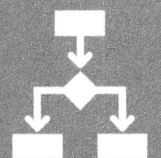

#4. Pedagogy
The alignment of the four features pedagogy (i.e. curriculum, teaching, learning, and assessment) is of utmost importance in pedagogical models.

Figure 3.1 A practice architecture of a pedagogical model

A practice architecture of the practising model

#1. Main Idea
An acceptance of better and worse ways of doing things

#2. Critical Elements
agency, content, goal, verticality, effort, uncertainty, and repetition.

#3. Learning Aspirations
acknowledging subjectivity and providing meaningful challenges, focussing on content and the aims of practising, specifying and negotiating stands of excellence, and providing adequate time for practising.

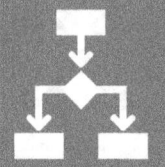

#4. Pedagogy
Stimulate and facilitate practicing and find ways to help student find an interest in practising. Provide meaningful and well-adapted challenges that help students, on an individual level, work in the space between 'I can' and 'I cannot'

Figure 3.2 A practice architecture of the practising model

A practice architecture of sport education

#1. Main Idea
Develop players in the fullest and richest sense

#2. Critical Elements
Roles, seasons, affiliation, formal competition, record-keeping, festivity and a culminating event

#3. Learning Aspirations
Competent, literate, and enthusiastic players.

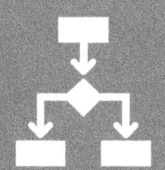

#4. Pedagogy
Enable students by developing a classroom environment that allowed for festivity and celebration and which assessed competency, literacy and enthusiasm rather than skills and techniques.

Figure 3.3 A practice architecture of sport education

A practice architecture of TGfU

#1. Main Idea
The development of thinking players

#2. Critical Elements
student-centredness, modified games, and the setting of problems to be solved by the players

#3. Learning Aspirations
Three nested categories: individual, small group, and whole (modified) game

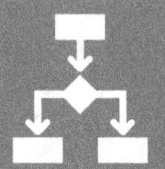

#4. Pedagogy
Teaching is facilitative, such as guided discovery (in Mosston's terms). Content will comprise both individual and team games, mostly in the form of games modified to match the learners' current readiness to learn.

Figure 3.4 A practice architecture of TGFU

A practice architecture of TPSR

#1. Main Idea
Learning life skills concerned with personal and social responsibility

#2. Critical Elements
Activities aimed at facilitating self and collective awareness, five levels of responsibility in action, times for reflection and decision-making about responsibility, and activities that develop respect, care and trust.

#3. Learning Aspirations
respect, participation, self-direction, caring, transferability

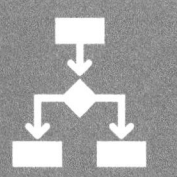

#4. Pedagogy
Curriculum content strongly influenced by pupil choice, and can either be group or individual activities. While the learning aspirations of this model are firmly in the affective domain,

Figure 3.5 A practice architecture of TPSR

A practice architecture of the activist model

#1. Main Idea
Learning to value the physically active life.

#2. Critical Elements
student-centredness, pedagogies of embodiment, inquiry-based education centred-in-action and listening to respond over time.

#3. Learning Aspirations
Girls' learning to name, critique, negotiate and, where possible, change barriers to their participation in physical activity.

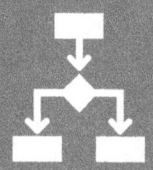

#4. Pedagogy
structured in-class discussions, visual methods such as drawing and photography, and the production, by pupils, of artefacts such as a book of games that girls can play.

Figure 3.6 A practice architecture of the activist model

A practice architecture of health-based PE

#1. Main Idea
Valuing movement

#2. Critical Elements
Teacher promotes meaningful physical activity; Teacher supports students to be informed movers; Teacher creates a needs-supportive learning environment; and Teacher encourages students to become critical movers

#3. Learning Aspirations
Habitual movers, motivated movers, informed movers and critical movers

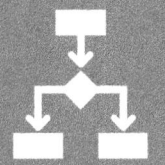

#4. Pedagogy
Teachers prioritize physical activity for life (2) changes require extended learning, (3) learning is meaningful and transferable, (4) develop intrinsic motivation for physical activity, and (5) programs should draw on multiple strategies.

Figure 3.7 A practice architecture of health-based physical education

A practice architecture of cooperative learning

#1. Main Idea
Learning with, by, from and for each other

#2. Critical Elements
Promotive face-to-face interaction, positive interdependence, individual accountability, small group and interpersonal skills and group processing

#3. Learning Aspirations
Togetherness, responsibility to self and others, communication skills, and feeling safe.

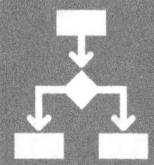

#4. Pedagogy
Putting cooperation ahead of skill development. Content would be devised to maximize student interactions and groups would be kept small enough to ensure that voice and choice were present.

Figure 3.8 A practice architecture of cooperative learning

and ideas. Either way, you are teaching using cooperative learning and your students are learning to be cooperative.

In an attempt to explain cooperative learning, we now unpack Figure 3.8. Starting with the *main idea*, you know you want students to *learn with, by, from and for each other*. Therefore, you need to map that out:

What does 'learning with' mean?

It means working in groups small enough so that everyone has a voice and can make an impact. This means avoiding close friends (as they can easily create a clique) or rivals (as this can cause unnecessary tensions).

Action: Select groups of about four or five where no one character dominates.

What does 'learning by' mean?

This means learning through the actual experience of cooperating. This may challenge young people to think about why their goals and the group's goals might align or might diverge. This type of thinking should challenge them to put the group before themselves.

Action: Develop tasks that rely less on personal success and more on whole group development. In this way everyone's learning is important.

What does 'learning from' mean?

This aspect of cooperative learning recognises that every student has prior experiences and valuable knowledge and that this can, and should, be an important aspect of group development.

Action: There is no one way of achieving success and everyone has a role to play in getting the group over the finish line. Therefore, focus more on the journey and less on the destination, and reward the steps to success as much as the success itself.

What does 'learning for' mean?

There are often aspects of physical education that we don't like and there are things that we don't want to do. There are also things that everyone finds challenging. 'Learning for,' therefore, is an acknowledgement that sometimes we need to do things because they benefit others and not just ourselves. Equally, we have to do things that provide a baseline or foundation for future development.

Action: Create challenges that require everyone to develop. 'One-size-fits-all' or ego challenges should be replaced with 'differentiated' or mastery challenges to ensure that everyone has somewhere to progress to.

The *critical elements* of cooperative learning provide its distinctive shape as well as give users some sense of what the creators regard as its unique and essential features. The critical elements of cooperative learning have been well explained elsewhere (see Dyson & Casey, 2016; Goodyear, 2013) but we have captured some of this thinking below.

Positive Interdependence: Success is achieved only in cooperative learning when students work together in teams and rely on each other to complete the task or win the game. Only in this way are students or players positively interdependent on each other. That is to say that students rely on each other to complete the pre-designed task. The idea of 'inter' (i.e., between) is key in this critical element. There must be dependency between individual students.

Individual Accountability: Students take responsibility for completing their part of the task for their group and learning something in the process. Students are assessed on their contribution to group work and their performance and not just for the completion of the task. In this way, students' contributions to the group's endeavours are seen to be on a par with the overall outcome. Consequently, the journey is as important as the destination.

Promotive Face-to-Face Interaction: Students develop and maintain positive interactions with members of their group. They should provide positive comments and engage in a supportive dialogue with other members of their group. The teacher should encourage students to listen to each of their team members during discussions and positively reinforce each other's performance.

Small-Group and Interpersonal Skills: These are student behaviours that allow comfortable and relaxed communication between group mates (i.e., listening, shared decision-making, taking responsibility, giving and receiving feedback, leading, following and encouraging each other). This is recognised through free and easy communication between groupmates.

Group Processing: The group reflects on what they have learnt and how they can improve their ability to work as a group. At the end of each lesson the team answers two questions: What went well in group work? and What does your group need to work on?

Learning aspirations are just that . . . aspirations. They are aspirations because the learning that results from students engaging in cooperative learning may not be immediately evident in the course or at the end of a unit. Outcomes suggest learning that is more convergent, tangible and immediate. Aspirations, in contrast, can be seen as being pliable, malleable and can be moulded to the local context and the reality of a given class on a given day (just like a ball of clay can be shaped). Meeting the learning aspirations involves differentiation in learning tasks, teaching styles and assessment practices.

In cooperative learning the learning aspirations are for *togetherness, responsibility to self and others, communication skills* and *feeling safe*. The central idea of learning aspirations for pedagogical models is that they are specific to the model, in ways that sports skills and Moderate to Vigorous Physical

Activity (MVPA) are not specific in multi-activity approaches (Casey & Kirk, 2021). These aspirations are things that you, as teachers, should be able to notice and are things you should look for.

The *pedagogy* of cooperative learning relates to teaching, learning, curriculum and assessment. As a teacher you will be striving to teach cooperation, and this means that you will place cooperation ahead of skill development. Students are learning how to work together in groups. Consequently, you will be seeking to maximise student interactions and these interactions can be rewarded and assessed. The curriculum will be designed to afford students chances to:

> (i) value both their own and others' contributions, (ii) become increasingly self-sufficient, (iii) adapt peer teaching to suit their own and others' needs, and (iv) think of ability in terms of contribution and not just performance.
> Casey and Fernandez-Rio (2019, p. 14)

Significantly the pedagogy in different classes, different schools and different school years are likely to look different depending on the young people and their learning needs.

What would sport education or the activist model look like if you applied the same process to their respective representations? Give it a go yourself and see if you can map it out. We have given this a start below.

The main idea of *sport education* is to develop students in the fullest and richest sense. This means that authentic participation in both the meaning and the rhythm of a sport season is important. Authentic experiences lie at the heart of sport education, and these should be at the heart of what you plan (Siedentop et al., 2004). The main idea of the *activist model*, in contrast, is valuing the physically active life. This means that young people can find opportunities to be active. They make individual and collective decisions to be active at times when it is not always easy or convenient. Providing opportunities in lessons to be active is about as convenient as it gets, and yet some young people might still choose not to be involved. The challenge, as we see it, is how to create an environment where not only do they see the value in activity but also choose to be active. How do you help them to carry those choices into recess or spaces out of school and how do you help them to be active?

TASK: Can you continue this and map out the critical elements, learning aspirations and pedagogy of these two models? What might this look like in your school?

Building the foundations

There are many ways to start with MbP. Our advice though is to start small and try to recognise the things you value or would like to value in physical education. Do not start with your curriculum (the here and now), but try and think about the one thing, or the handful of things, that are non-negotiable in your curriculum. As part of the collaborative process we outline in Chapters 4 and 5, now talk to colleagues and ask them to do the same. Your answer or answers may match or differ from theirs. But this does not matter. You are trying to gauge what is so important in your thinking about physical education that you will not compromise. This might be the engagement of all students in all lessons. Or the aspiration that all students will lead a healthy, active life. It might be that the achievements of all students are recognised and not just those who are seen to be able. Now compare it to your curriculum or your departmental timetable and try and recognise where this one thing or handful of things are represented in what you do in physical education. Now ask yourself if your students would recognise these things. Could they tell you what you value or would they be a million miles away? Since they too are key stakeholders in the school's physical education program, ask them and see if you are right.

In doing all of this, you might begin to recognise the practice architecture of physical education in your school and/or department. These are the practices that shape physical education but which, equally can be shaped, adapted and changed in response to our aspirations and actions.

What are the practice architectures in your school/department?

There are certain 'things' in your school that prefigure, predict and strongly suggest what can be done in physical education. These are the practice architectures, and they help us to see schools and classrooms as both pre-designed and situated in time and history. These are the things that are said about physical education (the sayings); that is, "we are a football/soccer school, we give students a variety of experiences so they can choose the one that's best for them." These are the things that are done in physical education (the doings), that is, "we use a multiple activity, sports skills approach when teaching physical education, we focus on moderate to vigorous physical activity." And these are the perceptions of, and policies in, the school that impact on what can happen in physical education (the relatings); that is, "physical education is a place where teachers tell students what to do and seek to ensure that students have the skills and knowledge to participate in the community."

Too often practice is preconfigured, rather than being aspirational. As a consequence, this predetermined approach to what is done in physical education limits what can be achieved. When people talk about physical education, and when they think about physical education in predictable ways, they impact on what physical education can be at any given time. The nature of physical education is influenced by both the environment in which it takes place and the individuals participating in it. The spaces where physical education occurs and the personal elements that individuals bring to it collectively shape what is permissible and achievable in physical education. Some practices are more plausible (e.g., basketball on a basketball court with basketballs) than others (parkour in the playground). Resources also predetermine what should and should not be done (it makes sense to play basketball because we have the space, the equipment and the knowledge). Finally, the way that practice connects people, the ways in which these people connect to practice and who holds power over these practices can have a strong influence over what is practised in the name of physical education and what is recognised as acceptable practice. If, for example, we went to school and associated physical education with traditional team games but came to your classes and saw yoga, then our relationship with your version of physical education would, in all probability, be skewed. If we held power, then we could 'make' you change the ways in which you practice. In other words, physical education is too often constrained by predetermined approaches rather than being aspirational. The predetermined nature of practices limits what is achievable and desirable in physical education. In short, the way people talk about and think of physical education impacts what it can become. The environment, individual participants, available resources and power dynamics all contribute to shaping what is permissible and achievable in physical education. These are 'things' that you need to be aware of if you want to adopt MbP and change what happens in physical education.

Despite the existence of practice architectures, they are often hidden, and, consequently, many of the preconfigured practices that shape physical education go unseen and unnoticed. The timetable, the geography of the school, the topics we teach and others often go unchanged for years and, in doing so, become the dominant ways of saying, doing and relating in physical education (see Casey & Kirk, 2021, for a fuller exploration). When trying to change and challenge any practice architectures, we first must notice and confront them and the part they play in the practice of physical education in our school. Do we recognise the impact of the timetable on physical education? Do we recognise the impact of the inter-school fixture list or inter-house events on physical education? Do we let district athletics or half-terms shape our physical education provision?

- What are the sayings, doings and relatings that influence physical education in your school/setting?
- Are these of your making or did you inherit them?
- Are they still relevant?
- Do they come true or are they just words?
- How do they relate to the one thing or things you noted earlier?

The sequencing of pedagogical models in MbP

Once you begin to see and understand the practice architecture of physical education in your school, you then need to decide on what you will do with this knowledge. In reading this book, you are thinking about introducing some pedagogical models to your school but which ones and with whom (i.e., which staff and which students)?

You have some choices to make. Do you start small with one class or a little bigger with one-year group? Do you have one topic/focus? Do you choose an established model/models for your first MbP undertaking? Sport education, for example, has had the most written about it, and there is a wealth of resources freely available on the Internet about this model. Teaching games for understanding, and other game-centred approaches, and cooperative learning are also well-resourced and researched approaches. They have been used in physical education over a number of decades, and lots of materials are readily available to help you as you start out. In contrast, the activist approach and the practising model are currently less well-used and resourced but that does not mean that there is no help or support available. There are lots of ideas in the public domain, but there just is not as much as for other models.

Remember that we are proposing MbP as an overarching idea that brings more than one pedagogical model into play to construct school physical education programs. In doing this we positioned the pedagogical model as the organising centre for MbP physical education. As such, you need to consider what you want it to *organise* from the start. Is it, for example, game play and tactics? Or cooperation and personal responsibility? Do you want to encourage and enhance girls' participation and move away from fitness testing? These combinations will allow you to choose your sequencing of models to best suit the needs of your students (see Table 3.1).

Let's imagine that you plan for your first use of MbP to fit into the existing multi-activity approach in your school. Therefore, instead of your normal six

Table 3.1 Aligning your focus to the chosen model

Focus 1	Focus 2	Model 1	Model 2
Game play	Tactics	Sport education	Game-centred approaches
Cooperation	Personal responsibility	Cooperative learning	Teaching personal and social responsibility
Girls' participation	Not fitness testing	Activist approach	Health-based physical education

Preparing to Succeed with MbP 45

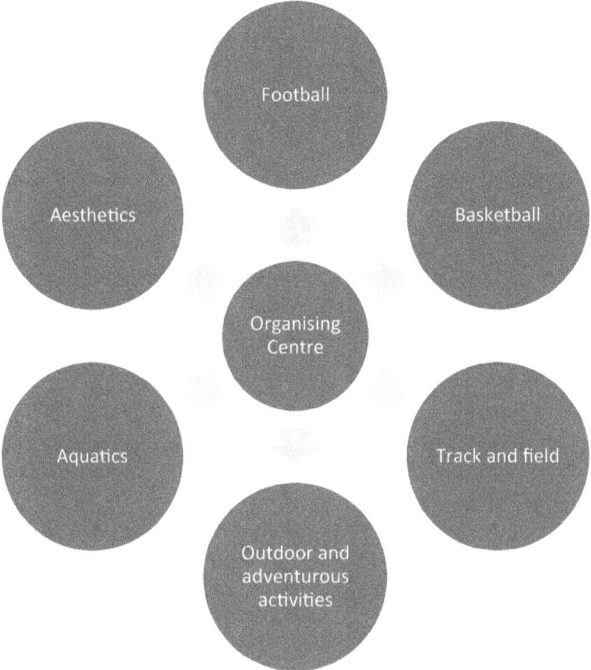

Figure 3.9 A multi-activity approach to the 11–12-year-olds' curriculum

blocks/units of work (see Figure 3.9), you decide to make some changes (see Figure 3.10) to the organising centre of physical education.

In the example above, Aesthetics (often seen as gymnastics and dance in many schools) has been replaced by cooperative learning as the organising centre of the unit. That does not mean that you will stop teaching Aesthetics, but your main idea, critical elements, learning aspirations and pedagogy, will shift. You will probably shift your approach to promote collaboration, independence, and flexibility and shift your perspective from individual achievement to collective progress. This might be through the vehicle of dance, but these aspirations will be your priority. Equally, in organising your unit around sport education, you will focus on developing competent, literate and enthusiastic sportspeople in the fullest and richest sense rather than focusing on the skills and techniques of basketball, even though basketball is the medium through which you utilise sport education.

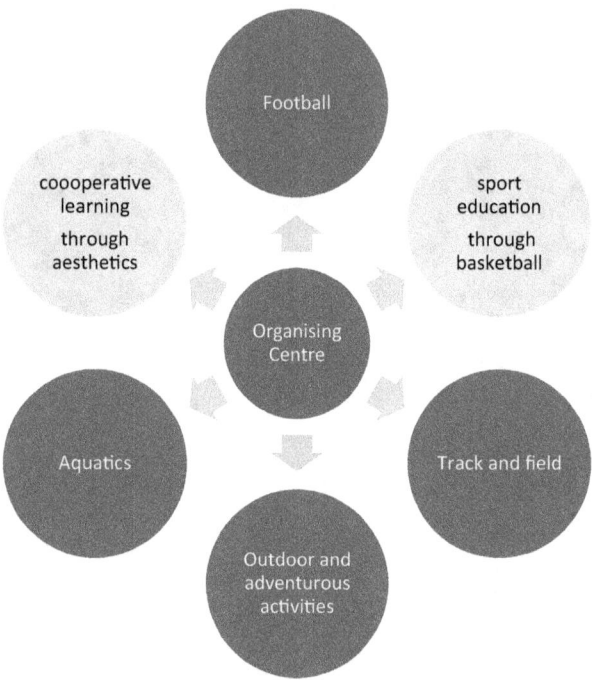

Figure 3.10 The use of two models in a multi-activity 11–12-year-olds' curriculum

Conclusion

A key message across this chapter has been to take it slow. The first time(s) you move away from your established physical education pedagogy and try something new you will make mistakes. This is not a simple undertaking. Things will go wrong and, as Ash's research and experiences show, you may feel like a beginning teacher again. That is to be expected and discomfort is part of the pedagogical learning process. Remember that you're learning to teach in a new way, and with that learning come mistakes and frustrations. They are to be expected. Embrace them. Be confident that these approaches work and can really engage and develop the young people in your care. But also remember that learning takes time. You have had to do it, we are sure, in many aspects of your life, so why not in your teaching?

Remember also that you need to recognise both the practice architectures in your school and department and your non-negotiables (more of this in the next chapter). What must, without compromise, be an outcome of your program? If it is that young people "value the physically active life" (Siedentop,

1996, p. 266), then are you achieving that? And how can MbP help you to achieve this goal better? If it is that you are state/county/national champions, then MbP may not be for you. But that's fine. We are not advocating MbP as the solution to every pedagogical change discussion. Rather it's an approach that has been shown to be very successful in multiple contexts.

Ultimately this chapter, and this book, has been written to help you in preparing to succeed with MbP. It has set out several steps you could follow to achieve this aim. It suggests that you take it slowly, maybe follow the simplest path, conduct a reconnaissance of your physical education offering and prepare the ground for success. The final decision on how to do this is up to you. Local agency is, after all, a key facet of MbP and one you should employ as you are the expert in your local context and know more about the young people in your care than either of us will ever know. That said, you have got this far. Why not pick a starting point and give it a go? What could possibly go wrong?

References

Casey, A. (2014). Models-based practice: Great white hope or white elephant? *Physical Education and Sport Pedagogy*, *19*(1), 18–34.

Casey, A., & Fernandez-Rio, J. (2019). Cooperative learning and the affective domain. *Journal of Physical Education, Recreation & Dance*, *90*(3), 12–17. https://doi.org/10.1080/07303084.2019.1559671

Casey, A., Fletcher, T., Schaefer, L., & Gleddie, D. (2017). *Practitioner research in physical education and youth sport: Reflecting on practice*. Routledge.

Casey, A., & Kirk, D. (2021). *Models-based practice in physical education*. Routledge.

Curtner-Smith, M. D., Hastie, P. A., & Kinchin, G. D. (2008). Influence of occupational socialization on beginning teachers' interpretation and delivery of sport education. *Sport, Education and Society*, *13*(1), 97–117. https://doi.org/10.1080/13573320701780779

Curtner-Smith, M. D., Kinchin, G. D., Hastie, P. A., Brunsdon, J. J., & Sinelnikov, O. A. (2021). "It's a lot less hassle and a lot more fun": Factors that sustain teachers' enthusiasm for and ability to deliver sport education. *Journal of Teaching in Physical Education*, *40*(2), 312–321.

Dyson, B., & Casey, A. (2016). *Cooperative learning in physical education and physical activity: A practical introduction*. Routledge.

Goodyear, V. A. (2013). *Participatory action research: Challenging the dominant practice architectures of physical education* [Unpublished PhD thesis, University of Bedfordshire]. Retrieved November 30, 2023, from https://uobrep.openrepository.com/bitstream/handle/10547/297585/goodyear.pdf?sequence=1

Kemmis, S., & Grootenboer, P. (2008). Situating praxis in practice: Practice architectures and the cultural, social and material conditions for practice. In S. Kemmis & T. J. Smith (Eds.), *Enabling praxis: Challenges for education* (pp. 37–62). Sense.

Siedentop, D. (1996). Valuing the physically active life: Contemporary and future directions. *Quest*, *48*(3), 266–274. https://doi.org/10.1080/00336297.1996.10484196

Siedentop, D., Hastie, P. A., & van der Mars, H. (2004). *Complete guide to sport education*. Human Kinetics.

Zhao, W. (2020). Epistemological flashpoint in China's classroom reform: (How) can a "Confucian do-after-me pedagogy" cultivate critical thinking? *Journal of Curriculum Studies*, *52*(1), 101–117. https://doi.org/10.1080/00220272.2019.1641844

4 Working collectively and collaboratively

A little help from your friends

The importance of collaboration and collective effort when implementing Models-based Practice in physical education

There are currently no *published* examples, to our knowledge, of a school adopting a Models-based Practice (MbP) approach to physical education. That said, we are aware of schools, in both the UK and internationally, that are currently implementing an MbP approach in their physical education provision and hope to play a role in bringing those examples to a wider audience.

We are aware, however, of one example in the literature of a teacher (Ash) adopting an MbP approach in physical education. He has claimed, and would still claim, this was a success. That said, he would also say that he did not always do it the easy or simple way. There are many reasons for this but the biggest was probably his isolation as a practitioner. He had little or no support – indeed interest – from most of his colleagues in MbP. Most did more to hinder him than they did to support him in this endeavour. That is not to say that they were deliberately unsupportive; this would suggest that they went out of their way to stop him. Which they didn't. It is more that some were passive aggressive. These colleagues questioned this way of teaching physical education. For them, the multi-activity approach, with its focus on skills and techniques, and the school's drive for inter-school sporting success were the only ways of teaching and structuring physical education they recognised and valued. Using MbP meant that Ash "wasn't teaching right" in their eyes, and he was told as much.

This meant that he had to do everything himself. He as good as hid his MbP approach from his colleagues. He used pedagogical models with the groups he taught on his own. He created boundaries around his work, and while he let people in to see what he was doing (people who often came from outside the school, or at least outside the physical education department), his work in MbP was tolerated by his colleagues rather than being embraced. While this worked, it wasn't ideal. All the ideas were his and his use of models was limited to what he could think up. He had help but that came from outside of physical education (from Anne-Marie Tarter, the school librarian)

DOI: 10.4324/9780429347078-4

and from outside of the school. Help came from his PhD supervisors (David, Anne Campbell and Belinda Cooke), his critical friends (Ben Dyson, Antonio Mendez and Peter Hastie) and from the literature he read daily. This was the only way MbP was going to work and yet, despite the barriers, the seven years in which he used MbP were the best of his teaching career. But they were challenging years and there was little or no longevity to MbP in the school. No one asked him for his lesson plans and schemes of work when he left. MbP, he suspects, left with him, and the classes he had taught reverted to a traditional approach to teaching and learning in physical education.

It would have been easier to have made these changes with company and support. That's not to say that, with company and support, MbP would have looked the same in the school. Other people's ideas and other people's motivations would have changed what happened, but they would have shared the burdens and the successes and maintained the momentum when Ash left the school. Even if a couple of colleagues were sympathetic to his vision (and one did but she arrived in his last year of teaching at the school and by that stage it was too late), then things might have been different. That said, what he achieved is to be celebrated and shows what can happen with a lot of personal drive, motivation and learning.

Given these experiences we advocate collaborative change while recognising what can be achieved in isolation. Our advice is to try and bring someone with you (ideally everyone in your department) but know that change is possible even when you have no internal collaborators.

Building a shared vision and understanding of MbP among educators

An MbP approach, as we have said in other parts of the book, takes time to develop. You would be poorly advised if we told you to choose MbP and run with it. When asked for advice about adopting an MbP approach to teaching physical education, we say, first and foremost, do not try to do too much. The first step is to decide what MbP means to you (as teachers, as a department and as a school). Changing physical education is something that will impact the practice architectures of physical education (see Chapter 3) and will change (a) what is said about physical education, (b) what is done in physical education and (c) the way the school communicates about physical education to its students, its parents and its governing body/administrators. That takes collective thought and action.

Our advice is to start with your ideas about what MbP is and how it will change physical education in your practice and your department's practice. Think about:

1. What MbP will allow you to do in physical education that you do not already do?
2. Why MbP will be better than what you already do?

3. How MbP will change physical education?
4. When MbP will first be implemented?
5. Where MbP will first be used?

Answering these questions – and other what, why, how, when, where and with who questions – will help you to have discussions with colleagues about your MbP vision for physical education. They will also serve as prompts for further reading and discussions.

Once you have had the first discussion – this might be with a colleague or an administrator – and you have made your case for MbP, then ask others to answer the same what, why, how, when, where and with who questions as you answered. Give them this book to read to see if they buy into these ideas. If they do, then what are their what, why, how, when and where statements? How do their answers interact or intersect with yours, and how might this ultimately change how MbP is enacted in your school?

A common goal for using pedagogical models (the organising centre of MbP) and MbP is to reach all the students in each class or school. Not just the highest-achieving students (who, truth be told, would probably excel regardless of your curriculum) but also the lower-achieving students. These are the young people who are most likely to be disconnected from your current physical education offering. But what if that's not the aim of your colleague or colleagues? Instead, they want to improve the cognitive or affective learning of all the children. How does this goal correspond with your aspirations? You both want physical education to have different practice architectures (i.e., sayings and doings), but they do not appear to immediately align. In this case, you need to do some more thinking and engage in further discussion.

Given that you want to connect students with physical education and your colleague(s) wants to improve their learning in the cognitive and affective learning domains, you may want to adopt a practising approach (see Figure 4.1). This model stimulates and facilitates practising and recognises that there are better and worse ways of doing things. Young people need to be provided with (or should provide their own) challenges. Maybe they wish to learn to juggle, or do a handstand, or perform an ollie on a skateboard. Whatever challenge they have, they (through you) will now use physical education time learning how to do this. This will require them to challenge their own thinking and recognise the feelings they experience during physical education. This might provide a close approximation of the sayings and doings each of you wanted to see in a new version of physical education. Regardless, and as Baker et al. (2023, p. 17) wrote, "it takes time to reconsider and ultimately change pedagogical practice. Be kind to yourself and your students by taking time to make the unfamiliar familiar."

A practice architecture of the practising model

#1. Main Idea
An acceptance of better and worse ways of doing things

#2. Critical Elements
agency, content, goal, verticality, effort, uncertainty, and repetition.

#3. Learning Aspirations
acknowledging subjectivity and providing meaningful challenges, focussing on content and the aims of practising, specifying and negotiating stands of excellence, and providing adequate time for practising.

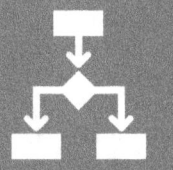

#4. Pedagogy
Stimulate and facilitate practicing and find ways to help student find an interest in practising. Provide meaningful and well-adapted challenges that help students, on an individual level, work in the space between 'I can' and 'I cannot'

Figure 4.1 A practice architecture of the practising model

Establishing a collaborative culture within the school or department

You have started to develop your initial concept for the MbP approach your school/department will undertake. Now it's time to bring these plans to the start line. If you know what you want to achieve, then align your ideas with one pedagogical model or many. If you can't do that, then pick the models first and pick out the aspects of each model that work for you. Which of the main ideas and critical elements best allow you to achieve the changes you want? Once you know, give them a go.

> Mark this page and go back to Chapter 3 and look at Figures 3.1 to 3.7. Perhaps you want students to learn life skills concerned with personal and social responsibility (teaching personal and social responsibility) or accept that there are better and worse ways of practising (practising model) or you want them to develop as thinking players (teaching games for understanding). Perhaps you consider these to be nice 'things' for your students to do but don't connect well with your what, why, how, when, where and with who answers from earlier in the chapter. If that is the case, then look at the main idea of other models and try to make those connections. Again, if there is no connection to be made, then you may need to look in another direction. One that might not be MbP.

In many of the schools we've worked with this is what we've recommended. Start with something. Pick a lesson, pick some part of a model, and give it a go. Perhaps it's the critical elements of positive interdependence and individual accountability from cooperative learning. Perhaps it's the levels of responsibility from TPSR, or competence and literacy from sport education, or inquiry-based education centred-in-action from the activist approach. Whatever it is, get together and plan a lesson or a part of a lesson. Collaborating with colleagues to plan, design and adapt pedagogical models has proven successful in many of the schools we've worked with. When colleagues share resources, ideas and experiences related to MbP, they find many connections and lots of things to talk about.

Once you've given it a go take the time to reflect on what happened. We bet it will be challenging. You will expect some of the reasons for this, but we wonder if there might be a few reasons you might not have expected. First, there will be many things that you feel you've gotten wrong, and this will play on your mind a little. Second, we expect that this will be one of the best planned lessons you taught for a while. We've seen it before. Teachers, like Ash, using cooperative learning for the first time, have a tendency to put every bit of their usual teaching down on paper for their students to follow. This often makes them feel that they have done their job as they learn to be a teacher in the somewhat strange new world they are creating around themselves. Third, the students have been both a little confused with what's happening and have done things that you didn't think they were capable of doing.

54 Working Collectively and Collaboratively

Finally, you have been caught in moments of indecision. You just didn't know how to respond to a particular situation or were second-guessing yourself. It's like being a beginning teacher again and it's not comfortable. Yes, you're excited about the possibilities but are a little baffled by the next decision you need to make. You might normally be thinking four moves ahead of yourself but it's not so easy now. In some cases, the next step is quite a challenge.

If you go through this on your own, it can be daunting but doing it collectively gives you support, criticality, challenge and a good dose of reality. Working with teachers and in teacher education for as long as we have, you realise that many teachers are their own worst critics. Probably not all teachers, or we wouldn't have the sayings, doings and relatings that we do in physical education, but many teachers. You want to do a good job, and pedagogical change can make you feel like that's not happening, but working collaboratively can not only keep you grounded but also help you to recognise the positive steps you are taking. Developing a collaborate culture stops you from getting ahead of yourself and doubting yourself. Sense checking and idea bouncing are just two of the advantages of changing your practice together.

Collaborative problem-solving and troubleshooting to address challenges and barriers

One of the cornerstones of MbP research is the idea that there is no one way of teaching physical education. Another cornerstone is there is no one way of using pedagogical models. It stands to reason, therefore, that there is no one way of developing an MbP approach. It takes time, collaborative problem-solving and lots of troubleshooting. How do you move towards MbP, and how do you keep going in a collectively agreed direction? Physiology indicates that if you close your eyes and try and walk in a straight line, you will invariably end up going around in a circle. Turning full circle is often the easiest outcome with any form of pedagogical change and you need to be mindful of it throughout the implementation process which may, as we have said early on, take a while.

So how do you manage this?

Each December lots of space in magazines, newspapers and social media posts is dedicated to New Year resolutions. Consequently, many people set off every January with good intentions to make wholesale changes to diets and exercise plans, but these good intentions can quickly waiver when faced with temptation, hunger and/or fatigue. At the same time of the year, we also hear that you shouldn't deprive yourself of your favourite treats or meals if you are trying to change the way you look. Nor should you overexercise. Rest is a vital part of any exercise plan. The same goes for MbP.

You should start by changing a few things. Start with those things about your practice that are the most disconnected from where you want to go and what you want to achieve. What, for example, is the one thing you can change that will make the biggest difference? What can you achieve if you start to make this aspect of your role better? Above, we have talked about your what, why, how, when, where and with who questions. Which of these stands out the most? Which is your biggest potential win?

Once you know the answer to these questions, then try and pinpoint what the one thing is you could change to make the biggest difference. Then think about what things stand in the way of you making that one big change. Knowing what your easy wins are and acknowledging your biggest challenges will help in your aim to change your practice.

You might, for example, acknowledge that the one thing you want to do is change the physical education offering for your oldest students. This might be the 11-year-olds or the 16-year-olds. Changing one of the things you do would be a step towards making that change. One of the barriers we have seen to MbP, however, is the perception that certain groups of children aren't ready for certain models because they lack the relevant skill set and/or attributes. So instead of changing the offering for your oldest students, you might change the offering for your second oldest students to prepare them for the changes you really want to make when they become the oldest students next academic year.

We have seen this work in several different contexts. Ash started his MbP approach with the youngest students in the school. He felt that they were the best behaved and most compliant students, and his pedagogical change would impact on him (as he was changing what he did in physical education) more than it would on them (who had never had a specialist physical education teacher before and who didn't know what physical education was in a secondary school context). It was only later that he sought to change the curriculum offering for the older students, and this, as he has argued elsewhere (see Casey & MacPhail, 2018), was harder teaching then with the younger students.

A similar approach has been taken in an English secondary school which, on Ash's advice, chose to introduce an MbP from the bottom of the school upwards. They are now in their third year of this change and three whole-year groups are now enjoying an MbP approach in all their physical education lessons. The school has seven classes in each year group and all students in the first three years of the school have been taught through models like sport education, health-based physical education, games sense and personal and social responsibility.

By doing this the teachers involved have identified their biggest aims/wins and have overcome some significant barriers. In Ash's case he did this alone, but in this case they achieved this as a department (which has contained eight different staff over the three years of implementation). All have been involved in the changes and all have had a contribution to make. This, we think, has been a major key in their development of an MbP approach.

56 Working Collectively and Collaboratively

Engaging in professional learning communities and networks to support implementation

We are confident that there are an increasing number of teachers and physical education departments looking to adopt MbP. The challenge is finding them and engaging with them. But where to look?

There has been a lot of engagement in pedagogical models through national PE associations. The Society for Health and Physical Education (SHAPE America in the USA), the Association for Physical Education (afPE in the UK), Physical Education Association of Ireland (PEAI), the Australian Council for Health, Physical Education and Recreation (ACHPER), Physical and Health Education Canada (PHE Canada) and the Scottish Association of Teachers of Physical Education (SATPE), among many others, have all engaged with MbP in some way or another. As national organisations they serve as important conduits to both innovative pedagogy and those who advocate such endeavours. Through their national and state conferences and publications, they have been responsible for the dissemination of research papers and practical ideas relating to MbP.

Beyond this there are many individuals who have engaged with and are willing to share information about pedagogical models and MbP. Social media, such as X/Twitter, Facebook, Instagram and LinkedIn, are great places to start your search for like-minded practitioners. In addition, of course, to national and state conferences and practitioner-focused publications like *PE Matters* (UK) and the *Journal of Physical Education, Recreation and Dance* (USA).

Involving students in the process through student voice and empowerment

'Student voice' is an increasingly familiar term in schools. In the UK, at least (and to the best of our knowledge), student panels are not uncommon in the recruitment of new teachers to a school. Equally, student opinion is frequently sought when developing the curriculum of the older students in the school. This is especially prevalent in England. For example, the key stage four offering has been recognised as a place where students (especially girls) have become increasingly disconnected and disaffected by the curriculum offered. This especially is the case when students reach the 14–15- and 15–16-year-old age groups. As such schools are asking students to make choices about what they want to do and are running recreational groups alongside more competitive offerings.

Whatever the reason for including students in decision-making in schools, it seems like an inherently good idea. Students are, after all, the reason why we do this. A school would be a purposeless place without the young people.

In several pedagogical models, student choice and student voice are inherent in the learning aspirations of the model. Take, for example, the activist model. The model aspires that girls will learn to name, critique, negotiate and, where possible, change barriers to their participation in physical activity. This can't be achieved without the teacher empowering the girls to have a central voice in the conceptualisation, construction and enactment of the physical education curriculum. Similarly, teaching personal and social responsibility seeks to help learners develop their respect, participation, self-direction, caring and the transferability of their learning between different contexts.

In both examples, and there were others we could have used, student voice is central to any modicum of success. Remember, not only are you learning to teach in a new way but the students are learning to learn in a new way. The feedback loop that can be created by allowing your students to input into the change process shouldn't be ignored. That said, and as Rudduck and Flutter (2000, p. 83) warned, "it takes time and very careful preparation to build a climate in which both teachers and students feel comfortable working together on a constructive review of aspects of teaching, learning and schooling."

When Ash was shifting towards MbP he used comment cards as a tentative mechanism to involve his students in the study and as a means of reassuring them that his intentions were honourable. He decided that comment cards, in the form of small pieces of brightly coloured pieces of card (see Figure 4.2) afforded him the chance to build regular consultation with his students into his lessons. Once in possession of the feedback, he was able to use the feedback to make immediate modifications as appropriate without further recourse to his students.

This initial and restrained period of PhD data gathering served to reassure the students that they could say anything they wanted about his teaching – good or bad – provided it was polite and they used a 'what and why' format in their responses. The cards were about 6 cm long and 2.5 cm wide and had space for the student's form group and a comment. They were left in the changing rooms, and after writing, the students could leave them in a sealed box for Ash to read later.

FORM:	DATE:
COMMENT:	
What?	
Why?	

Figure 4.2 Student comment card

This is an extract from Ash's thesis (Casey, 2010) that shows how these comment cards were used and how they impacted on his teaching and the co-construction of lesson and units of work.

The students started off with some terse replies – "easily understood; good liked it; good very helpful; it was good; learnt a lot" (Comment Cards, January 17, 2006) – which were pleasant to hear but which did not really help me. With patience and trust they started to produce comments that I could use to develop my pedagogy:

- It was a good idea but is quite hard to understand and should be explained more
- It was a good idea but didn't work that well
- It was a very good idea but hard to understand
- I liked it; it improved my swimming a lot already. I would like to always use the cards
- It was a good idea and I really enjoyed it but it could have been a bit harder
- I enjoyed it and thought it was really good because we were in the water a lot of the time!
- It was good for beginners but not for top group
- I thought it was good as I think it's better to get advice from fellow swimmers
- Cool it's nice and relaxing and you're learning how to swimming. Brilliant Teachers!
- Good but didn't understand what to do until the very end
- It was good to have something to work from. I thought they helped and would like to use them again
- I think that the pair-check sheets are good but would be better if we could write comments
- The sheet was very good because it told you how you should swim and it corrected how you swim
- It was useful because it showed you how to do breaststroke
- It was helpful but I personally didn't understand the boxes
- I liked being judged by my swimming friends
- The lesson looks good because it looked like they were having fun and it looked like they were learning (non-swimming coach)
- Quite complicated but the principal was there
- I felt that this lesson was an effective way of pair assessment it was a good way and I learnt a lot

Comment Cards (February 13–17, 2006)

> The comment cards proved to be a great way of allowing the students an anonymous and immediate impact on lessons (cooperative learning in this case). Furthermore, their observations were taken very seriously and often were the triggers for changes in my teaching. These initial attempts at asking for student opinion gave them the opportunity to express their opinions in a quick and anonymous way. These simple pieces of cards were used as a way of showing there were no repercussions (except positive change in lessons) from their comments and paved the way to more honesty in future discussions.

Inviting students to be involved wasn't a quick or easy process; it took a lot of time and energy (and led to a few unflattering and derogatory replies – all anonymous of course – when the older students got hold of the cards). That said, it was a gateway to change and a platform for trust. In the end Ash's students were co-investigators in his PhD and their voices were both valued and integral to his use of MbP. They became critical research participants, but it took time to build trust. There would have been little worse than a negative response by Ash to a comment or simply ignoring their comments altogether. This would have disempowered them, which was not his intention. Indeed, why take the time to engage with students if that engagement is only going to be belittled or ignored? Only by giving them value will students' voices become loud enough and astute enough to help you make the changes you have imagined.

This is especially important given what many see as the disconnect between school physical education and children's interests. For example, in a recent paper O'Connor et al. (2022) set out to rethink the four established classifications of games (i.e., target, net/wall, striking/fielding and invasion) and proposed that a wider range of forms of sport should be considered in physical education. They did this, we believe, because physical educators have thought in the same way about the core activities in physical education for too long. Participation and interest have changed, but physical education hasn't. It is important that we challenge the status quo and consider what is prevalent and relevant to young people in the 21st century. It is too easy to maintain the equilibrium, but it doesn't reflect what is happening in youth sport and leisure time around the globe. Only by stopping and thinking about what is current – and it here that student voice can really help us – can we begin to reframe physical education (perhaps through MbP) and re-engage many young people.

The result of O'Connor and colleagues' work was the addition of five game types: lap or circuit, route or journey, rush or action, stunts or tricks, and rhythmic sports, to the existing net/wall, invasion, target, and striking and fielding game types. Each of these new types was positioned to consider the social, environmental and affective dimensions of learning. One of the 'things' that was missing from this proposal, however, was the voice of young people. We wonder what these ideas would have looked like with the involvement of young people. Equally, we wonder what your physical education provision would look and feel like with the engagement of your students and their voices.

Reflecting on collective progress and making adjustments based on feedback and evidence

One of the cornerstones of change is evidence (and we will talk about this more in the next chapter). Conversely, one of the criticisms of physical education is that, as a subject, we do not evidence what works and what does not work, nor can we show the things that we tried to make improvements. If this was a school chemistry experiment, we would, we suspect, struggle to write up a lab report about teaching in physical education.

Yes, we have a lot of anecdotal evidence about our successes and failures but how much evidence could we provide if we were asked to prove our practices were effective? Probably not very much. But why would we? This is not the data that drives schools. The evidence of our worth as teachers often comes through league tables and they have no interest in our pedagogies. Instead, they care what student X remembered on day Y in their national qualification.

Now, you could take the same approach with your pedagogical change but it's a little too easy to skew the results or miss the little things. We have already written about the challenges of adopting an MbP approach to teaching physical education (see Casey & Kirk, 2021). As such, you may already be aware of what it will take for you to make the changes you had in mind when you picked up this book. But how will you show that you are making progress? Science tells us that our memories are fallible. We also already know that we are biased. Will you see things that never happened, or will you disparage a lack of change when change is actually happening? Are you a fan of this change or are you an opponent? Are you reading this book because you want to change or someone else has 'suggested' that you do? What outcome do you really want from this work?

Start there. Be honest with yourself at least. "I really want MbP to [succeed/fail] in the next [week/month/term/year/three years]." Giving yourself enough time to change is also important. We already know that resolutions are hard to keep. So be nice to yourself. Adopting an MbP approach overnight is not realistic unless you want to drop the idea by the end of day two. Instead, be realistic. "I want all the children to have experienced a sport education season by the end of this academic year" or "We will use the activist approach with all the middle school to senior classes and see what they prioritise for their learning."

In the previous section we talked about student voice, and this is a way of gathering evidence. In universities we often respond to student feedback with a 'you said, we did' poster. Could you do the same? This would be one way of collecting and collating the opinions we might gather from students. You could develop this to include a 'we did, you did' poster. This could map the things you did as a teacher or a department and the subsequent actions and reactions of your students. All of this would certainly be useful when explaining pedagogical change to other stakeholders with a vested interest in what happens in physical education. This is worth thinking about and we will continue to discuss this in Chapter 5.

Celebrating successes and recognising the contributions of all stakeholders in the implementation of MbP

In many schools in the UK, we have a sports day every year. Truth be told, this is not often a day but an afternoon. Also, it's not actually a day of sports as much as it is a couple of hours of track and field athletics. But that aside, it is often the one occasion in the school calendar when lessons are suspended and the whole school comes down to the track to watch the different events. Stereotypically the maths department keeps the records and the other departments take on a multitude of different roles from marshal to starter to place judge.

We used to love sports day but have since wondered why physical education is only really celebrated on one day every year. Why don't we celebrate our achievements more often, and why don't we recognise the success we have had, and the students have had? Often, we measure success in physical education by our results against local schools or in regional and national competitions. We frame the playing shirts of our alumni and hang them in the department but what about those whose biggest success was to swim 20 metres? Or develop enough self-confidence to attend the after-school program?

And what about you? Are your successes defined by what the tiny minority achieved or by what you do? Is following your beliefs and building and rebuilding the very best pedagogy you can ever be celebrated? It should be but you need to set yourself some goals and then tick them off. What will your success indicators look like, and how will the rest of the school know about them? We think it's time to start celebrating the small wins. Those that can be attributed to your teaching and not just through association.

Write down your goals and keep a record. Some might be easy wins, and some may be of a longer term. Talk about these with your department and administrators. We have been told that verbalising goals is a good way of helping yourself to bring them to fruition, so our advice is not to keep these aims to yourself. Share them with the world.

Conclusion

In the conclusion to a paper exploring steps and not just journeys in pedagogical change, Casey (2013) wrote:

> Sometimes the messiness needs to be recognised as being as important as the final change. Reflective odysseys clearly have a place in our literature but we also need to better understand how pedagogical change occurs. Unless we acknowledge that *pedagogical change takes time and is achieved over a number of individual steps*, rather than simply being a journey to celebrate, then we will continue to have an 'airbrushed' view of the destination, rather than understanding that difficult steps were required to reach it.
>
> Casey (2013, p. 161, emphasis added)

Given the messages in this chapter, indeed in the whole book, we draw your attention to the idea that *"pedagogical change takes time and is achieved over a number of individual steps."* Those steps can be taken alone or in collaboration with colleagues and/or students. Throughout this chapter we have emphasised the importance of collaboration and collective effort when implementing MbP in physical education. While 'going it alone' has proven successful in the past, this is by no means the preferred route. By collectively acknowledging the existence of potential barriers in your school, the decision to use MbP becomes more appealing and sustainable. By co-constructing your vision for physical education through MbP, developing your understanding and actioning a cultural shift within your school and/or department, the changes you envision for physical education can become more a reality and less an aspiration.

Through the chapter we have provided practical guidance on building this shared vision, establishing a collaborative culture, engaging in collaborative problem-solving and utilising professional learning communities to support MbP implementation. Furthermore, in emphasising the importance of involving students, we have provided an additional means of enhancing their learning experience and gaining valuable feedback on your endeavours. In the next and final chapter, we explore how you might go about making a case for MbP at the school level.

References

Baker, K., Scanlon, D., Tannehill, D., & Coulter, M. (2023). Teaching social justice through TPSR: Where do I start? *Journal of Physical Education, Recreation & Dance, 94*(2), 11–18.

Casey, A. (2010). *Practitioner research in physical education: Teacher transformation through pedagogical and curricular change* [Unpublished PhD thesis, Leeds Metropolitan University].

Casey, A. (2013). "Seeing the trees not just the wood": Steps and not just journeys in teacher action research. *Educational Action Research, 21*(2), 147–163. https://doi.org/10.1080/09650792.2013.789704

Casey, A., & MacPhail, A. (2018). Adopting a models-based approach to teaching physical education. *Physical Education and Sport Pedagogy, 23*(3), 294–310. https://doi.org/10.1080/17408989.2018.1429588

Casey, A., and Kirk, D. (2021). *Models-based practice in physical education.* London: Routledge.

O'Connor, J., Alfrey, L., & Penney, D. (2022). Rethinking the classification of games and sports in physical education: A response to changes in sport and participation. *Physical Education and Sport Pedagogy*, 1–14.

Rudduck, J., & Flutter, J. (2000). Pupil participation and pupil perspective: "Carving a new order of experience". *Cambridge Journal of Education, 30*(1), 75–89.

5 Making a case for MbP at school level

Introduction

We have suggested elsewhere in this book that, as you transition to MbP as an approach to practising physical education, you start with little things, involving small changes. But we also want you to think big. This is because MbP, if implemented fully, will radically change physical education in your school. As such, it will be important to have all the main stakeholders on your side from the beginning. Ash's story, as told in Chapter 4, is not the ideal way to go, with passive-aggressive colleagues taking unhelpful and unsupportive positions as he worked solo to change his practice. It is also possible that some of the pedagogical models you will want to implement have resource implications. Indeed, your transition to MbP will require the most precious resource of all for teachers, which is time. You will want to have the time you need to make a good job of MbP.

So what's involved in making a case for MbP at the school level? The first thing we need to recognise is that while good ideas are essential, they are not enough (Thompson & Purdy, 2017). Schools, like any other complex organisation, have their own micro-politics. Implementing MbP is a form of educational innovation, even when teacher-initiated (Kirk, 1986), and so it is important to recognise that there is a game to be played in persuading others that MbP is a good idea and that, moreover, it will be a significant change for the better in terms of benefitting your students.

There are at least three things to consider about this micro-political game. The first is the players, the groups of people who have a stake in physical education – in other words, the stakeholders. A second issue is preparing yourself as thoroughly as possible to be an advocate for MbP. Reading this book is, of course, a great starting point, but you also want to carry out a reconnaissance of your local context in order to better understand, among other things, the needs and interests of your key stakeholder, your students, as well as others' perspectives (see Chapter 4 for some more ideas). Finally, armed with good ideas and information, evidence of what works, how it works and why

DOI: 10.4324/9780429347078-5

it works will be essential in sustaining and further developing the transition to MbP. In the following sections we look at each of these issues in turn.

Stakeholders

Stakeholders are people who care about and are impacted by your work in physical education. There are at least four groups of stakeholders who have a direct interest in physical education in your schools: your students, their parents, your colleagues and your school leaders. Understanding the nature of the stake they hold in physical education, what they care about and how they might support your work in MbP is key to determining your success. Building trust and rapport is essential, though this will clearly take different forms with each group. At the same time, good communication will be important with each group. Communication isn't a one-off event but something that is ongoing; keeping channels open is central in sustaining and developing the implementation of MbP.

Your students are the number-one stakeholder in physical education. Consultation with students is surprisingly rare in physical education. However, some pedagogical models are explicitly student-centred, such as cooperative learning, activist approaches, sport education and teaching games for understanding. As such, teacher and student co-construction of physical education programs is required. Co-construction involves communication among teachers and students and active listening to respond on the part of the teacher (Oliver & Kirk, 2015). We know from the research literature that having choices is a powerful motivational tool, particularly in terms of fostering autonomous motivation (Van den Berghe et al., 2014).

Parents, the second group of stakeholders, can play a part in promoting MbP with their children. Parents' views of physical education are more often than not shaped by their own school experiences, and no doubt are as varied as your students' experiences. You may only see parents at occasional parents' evening, and they only make an appointment if there is a particular issue they want to discuss but that doesn't mean that they have no interest in the physical education experiences of their children. Given this, it may be necessary to use a number of avenues to communicate with parents about what you are planning and how MbP can benefit their children, including special information evenings and demonstration events, as well as any web-based communication systems your school has in place. In the case of parents with children in your school who value the traditional approach (often because this is what they remember from school themselves), you may need to make a case for why MbP is a valuable and meaningful approach to physical education. This is where gathering information from other schools and generating evidence (mentioned below) of your own practice will be important.

Colleagues, particularly those in physical education, are also key stakeholders. As already mentioned, the least supportive scenario is where colleagues are unwilling to join in with the transitional process to MbP and effectively act as barriers to change. Getting other teachers on-side would appear, at face value, to be a smart move. We wrote in Chapter 4 about the downside of trying to 'fly solo' and the importance of collaboration, preferably with those colleagues who are closest to the innovation action. At the same time, as Kirk's (1986) study of teacher-initiated innovation in physical education showed, it is possible to take a range of supportive roles that don't all require the same levels of time and commitment. You ideally want others' participation to be voluntary and based on a shared understanding of what MbP can achieve.

A fourth group is your head teacher or administrator and other school leaders who manage some aspects of your work. Aligning your goals for MbP with wider goals for the school will be important. So too will communicating the benefits of MbP in terms that are most likely to be understood by school leaders. They will play a part in providing approval and resources for undertaking MbP, but they can also become important advocates on your behalf across the school, to parents and also beyond the school. Evidence can be a powerful tool in gaining this support, something we will come to soon.

There may be others who can be considered stakeholders in your physical education program whom we haven't mentioned here but who are active in your own, specific, local context. Whoever they are, identifying key stakeholders will be an important early task in making the case for MbP. Discussing your plans with them will not only provide them with information but also allow you to refine your ideas and, possibly, even spark some new ones. Essential to this communicative effort will be your thoroughgoing knowledge of your local context through reconnaissance.

Reconnaissance

The notion of reconnaissance is borrowed from Kemmis et al. (2014) and their work on critical participatory action research (CPAR). While we are not advocating here that you need to engage in CPAR in order to implement MbP, there are processes they set out that are good practice in making a case for new practices. The notion of reconnaissance itself, reflecting its use in military contexts, is a preliminary exploration ahead of, and in order to inform, the main action to follow. It is, at heart, a shared, information-generating process.

According to Kemmis et al, the first and crucial phase is to open up a communicative space that they call "establishing the public sphere." By this they do not mean opening up your practice to the general public but, rather, establishing a reference group who will participate together in developing and implementing MbP. The stakeholders discussed earlier make obvious members of such a group. You may also seek additional members, if this is possible, for example, from neighbouring schools, your local authority and university, although this is not a requirement.

The public sphere is a space where communication between you and other stakeholders can occur. Not only can members of the group provide information from their perspective on your initial plans for MbP, they can also offer suggestions for how you might take these forward. This is particularly important in the early phase of adopting MbP, since it provides you with opportunities to learn from others about their perceptions of physical education and also for you to test the robustness of your ideas in conversation with others.

Once established, the public sphere becomes a communicative space in which you can develop a shared language about MbP. For example, it is a space to discuss how the practice architecture of pedagogical models may differ from current practice in terms of, for example, sayings, doings and relatings (see Chapter 3). It provides a medium for introducing key terminology such as pedagogical model, and the specific models you have been thinking about using. It has, then, a proactive purpose in the beginning to lay the foundation for what is to come.

Kemmis and colleagues recommend that before you move on from the reconnaissance phase you prepare, along with group members, an initial statement about what you, individually and collectively, intend to do. This statement serves a number of purposes. First, it brings together, in a succinct form, the output of the various conversations and discussions that have taken place. Second, it provides an accessible expression of what has been agreed about implementing MbP and the benefits the group believes will flow to stakeholders. Third, it becomes the starting point for the next phase of action. And fourth, it provides a means of measuring progress, a point of comparison between then and now, as MbP is rolled out in your physical education program.

The initial reconnaissance phase is integral to making a case for MbP because communication among key stakeholders takes place from the beginning and everyone, hopefully, feels they have had a say in what is to happen. As you begin to enact your plans, and as we wrote in Chapter 4, the generation of evidence of the effects of your innovative actions will be a central component in making and continuing to make the case for MbP.

The generation of evidence

The reconnaissance phase is, as we noted above, the foundation upon which MbP is built. The next phase, borrowing again from Kemmis et al. (2014), is the think-plan-act-observe-reflect cycle. Kemmis et al. (2014) use the plural to talk about a spiral of cycles since the process of implementing MbP will not have an endpoint, where everything is done. At the heart of this cycle of action is the generation of evidence, which is crucial to making the case for MbP.

We have suggested elsewhere in this book how you might go about planning MbP (see Chapter 4), including the length of units of work appropriate to the models being implemented, the sequencing of models and their interrelationships, teaching and learning strategies you plan to utilise, the actual content to be deployed and assessment practices.

Putting the plan into action is next within the cycle. Kemmis and colleagues recommend that you begin the process of 'observing' how the plan works relatively early, certainly within the first few weeks. They also recommend that you keep a field journal with dated entries in order to organise information used to make judgements about progress. We agree with this suggestion because gathering good evidence not only informs your decision-making but is also of great importance for making and maintaining your case for MbP within the reference group and beyond.

Evidence can take many forms. In addition to your own reflections, which we will return to momentarily, evidence can include outcomes of student assessment, perspectives of key stakeholders, video recording of lessons, photographs and other visual artefacts produced by students, just to mention a few. The evidence you generate and the methods you use to do this will very much link with the form of MbP you enact. The evidence should also be able to throw light on your initial statement of intent, which may have some mention of evidence already built into it.

Periodically in the think-plan-act-observe-reflect cycle, you will want to make time for reflection, individually and collectively. Reflection is focused on the evidence you have generated and can become another level of evidence in itself. Kemmis et al. (2014) suggest that reflection should focus on anticipated and unanticipated effects, intended and unintended effects, and side effects. The purpose of reflecting on the evidence you have marshalled has a main purpose, which is to inform what you do in the next think-plan-act-observe-reflect cycle. And making a case for what you do next with MbP is very much part of this process, where you return to your reference group and the public sphere to share the outcomes of reflection. Kemmis et al propose that these shared reflections should form the basis of a new statement of intent before the start of the next cycles of action.

A generation of evidence example

In the first empirical paper of its kind, Casey and MacPhail (2018) explored an MbP approach to physical education. Investigating a multi-year, multi-model, multi-class implementation of three pedagogical models (cooperative learning, sport education and tactical games), these authors scrutinised pedagogical change from the vantage point of an experienced practitioner researcher (Casey himself). Casey and MacPhail (2018) used the notion of model fidelity (Hastie & Casey,

2014) to provide a rich description of the curricular elements (i.e., the main idea, critical elements, learning aspirations and pedagogy) of the three models explored in this paper.

Digging deeper, and exploring each facet of practice architectures in turn, it is clear that Casey and MacPhail (2018) took a robust approach to positioning their work in the broader narratives of physical education and education. The *sayings* talked of agendas around student voice, the need to move beyond a single model and the need to help teachers (both pre-service and in-service) understand and gain experience and confidence in using multiple models in a program.

The authors argued that it was necessary to define the *doings* we aspire to in physical education and find approaches that best facilitate these ambitions. They position MbP as a way of "meaningfully and purposefully connect[ing] different models in a school's curriculum" (Casey & MacPhail, 2018, p. 296). This was partially achieved in the results of the paper through the teacher's "continually striving for high fidelity" and his "knowledge of his classes" (p. 302). In keeping with MbP, the researchers also reported on the teacher's predominantly partially successful attempts to reduce his involvement and grant the students ownership over their learning. Casey showed authenticity as a teacher by trying to "squeeze every drop of time from the lesson" (p. 305) and his vulnerability by "trying to achieve too much in the time he had" (p. 305).

The *relatings* of the study were used to show that the teacher's knowledge of both the class and the different pedagogical models was a strength of the curriculum. Casey and MacPhail (2018) acknowledged the importance of changing the power relationships in lessons and providing students with "the language and physical skills they would need to enact their roles effectively as well communicate with their peers and teacher" (p. 304). They also acknowledged the difficulties inherent in doing this and the amount of time required. Nevertheless, such a power shift changed the teacher's view of his students: "rather than products that I produce they are more like co-authors of their works" (p. 306).

Fundamentally, Casey and MacPhail (2018) positioned each model as a specification for practice and showed how the curriculum was tailored to the local context. Equally they showed how pedagogical models could both act as a new organising centre for program design and allow for the co-construction of physical education among teachers, students and other stakeholders. Nevertheless, while this work gives us our first empirical example of MbP, this was a rudimentary attempt – by the standard we aspire to in this book – that fitted into and around the multi-activity, sport technique-based approach to physical education that dominated the school's curriculum.

Conclusion

Our focus in this chapter has been making a case for MbP. As you can see, this is not a one-off event. Your advocacy for MbP is rooted in your actions, of consulting with your key stakeholders by opening up a 'public sphere,' of reconnaissance to learn more about your local context and the conditions that need to be in place for MbP to succeed, and in generating evidence of its effects.

You might start small as we have proposed, but you want to think big. MbP has the potential to radically alter your approach to physical education: we think for the better, in so far as *all* of your students can benefit from physical education. Working with the think-plan-act-observe-reflect cycle builds into your practice the generation of evidence on which to base further advocacy for MbP. And while publicising your innovative work with MbP may be well down your list of intentions to begin with, being able to provide evidence of what works beyond your immediate local context could make one small contribution to a bigger movement in physical education.

References

Casey, A., & MacPhail, A. (2018). Adopting a models-based approach to teaching physical education. *Physical Education and Sport Pedagogy*, *23*(3), 294–310.

Hastie, P.A., & Casey, A. (2014). Fidelity in models-based practice research in sport pedagogy: A guide for future investigations, *Journal of Teaching in Physical Education*. 33: 422 – 431.

Kemmis, S., McTaggart, R., & Nixon, R. (2014). *The action research planner: Doing critical participatory action research*. Springer.

Kirk, D. (1986). Temporal dimensions of an innovative idea: A case study of teacher-initiated innovation. *Journal of Curriculum Studies*, *18*(3), 311–330.

Oliver, K. L., & Kirk, D. (2015). *Girls, gender and physical education: An activist approach*. Routledge.

Thompson, T. A., & Purdy, J. M. (2017). When a good idea isn't enough: Curricular innovation as a political process. *Academy of Management Learning & Education*, *8*(2). https://doi.org/10.5465/amle.2009.41788842

Van den Berghe, L., Vansteenkiste, M., Cardon, G., Kirk, D., & Haerens, L. (2014). Research on self-determination in physical education: Key findings and proposals for future research. *Physical Education and Sport Pedagogy*, *19*(1), 97–121.

6 Conclusion

Introduction

In bringing this book to a close we wanted to offer a brief collective summary and an invitation (but more of that later). Across this book we have argued that MbP represents a significant shift from the traditional approach to teaching in physical education that Kirk (2013, p. 974) described as the "one-size-fits-all, sport technique-based, multi-activity form." By focusing on student-centric learning, the use of multiple pedagogical models and the importance of collaborative and reflective practice, MbP offers teachers and schools an alternative future for physical education. We've argued throughout for the transformative potential of MbP and emphasised the need for a patient, evidence-based approach to implementing pedagogical and curricular change in your particular educational setting. In what remains of the book, we summarise the first five chapters under five headings: (1) transformation through MbP, (2) multiple pedagogical models, (3) embracing change and challenges, (4) collaborative approach and advocacy and (5) evidence-based practice.

Transformation through MbP

We believe that MbP has the potential to revolutionise physical education. By shifting the organising centre away from sport-specific content to a wider pedagogy-centric approach, MbP helps you to promote an inclusive, student-focused, developmentally appropriate learning environment. MbP is anchored in the dynamic interplay of teaching, learning, curriculum and assessment and builds on the main idea, critical elements, learning aspirations and pedagogy of each model. It is both the complementary and contradictory practice architectures of different models that enable you to create a flexible and responsive program in your school. That said, it's not an instantaneous change but a slow conversion from where you are now to where you want to be.

To achieve this degree of change, you need to understand what your ambitions are and what your non-negotiables will be in terms of your school and

DOI: 10.4324/9780429347078-6

your offering. Once you know this you can set about the process of change. Don't overlook the importance of this step nor the amount of time this will take. The old analogy in DIY is measure twice and cut once. The same applies here. Have a firm understanding of where you want to go and then take those first steps.

Multiple pedagogical models

Once you know where you want to go you need to determine how. This will require the exploration and actualisation of various pedagogical models, both well-established and emerging. The existence of multiple models underscores the versatility of MbP. These models are characterised by their distinct main ideas, critical elements, learning aspirations and pedagogies. This diversity allows for the development of a tailored educational experience that moves beyond the traditional focus on sport techniques and games.

Some models will be easier to use than others. Some will better fit your own beliefs about physical education and your aims for the future. Equally, some are already better researched, and more resources can be easily sourced online or through professional and academic journals. Established models already exist in the wider world and other teachers have engaged with them. That said, be cautious of what you find online. As we have argued in this book, local agency is important, and you are the expert regarding your school and your students. So be prepared to tailor anything you 'import' into your practice.

Emerging models have the advantage of being fresh. You can learn about them and develop for your school without being overly influenced by what others have done before you. You can also be at the forefront of using these models, and we are sure that the individuals involved in developing these models would be interested to hear your thoughts and experiences of using the ideas and practices they are working with.

Embracing change and challenges

Throughout we have emphasised the importance of patience and resilience in the face of challenges when implementing new pedagogical methods. Learning from mistakes and embracing discomfort are crucial aspects of this journey. Things will be different when using MbP. That's the nature of change. Things won't always go according to plan either but that's also the nature of change.

Recognise the unique characteristics of your school environment. Aligning these characteristics with the practice architectures of both MbP and the pedagogical models you wish to use is important. Synergies and disconnection may not always be apparent, and you may try something or some things that don't work but that too is the nature of change. Try different things with different classes and different year groups and give yourself permission to fail. Equally, don't try to change everything. This is likely to end in either failure or a lot more work than perhaps you anticipated. This can be a reason for not changing in the long run.

Collaborative approach

The importance of collaboration in implementing MbP is a recurring theme in this book. Working together with colleagues and students can help in overcoming potential barriers and create sustainable and meaningful pedagogical change. Colleagues can help you advocate for change. The collective effort in building a shared vision for physical education through MbP can act as a catalyst for change. It can also reduce your individual workload as you spread the expertise and endeavour around. Having people to talk to, to share ideas with, tackle problems and share success has shown to be a very powerful way of engaging in change. Finding some allies and crucial friends is a well-established route to success. Going it alone can work, as we showed, but it's not the path of least resistance.

Advocacy and evidence-based practice

Finally, throughout the book we made a case for advocating MbP through consistent actions and evidence-based practices. This involves consulting key stakeholders, understanding the local context and generating evidence of MbP's effectiveness. The think-plan-act-observe-reflect cycle was given as an example of how you might develop a tried-and-tested approach to continuously improve and advocate for MbP. Self-advocacy – showing yourself your own successes and the steps you have taken to change your practice – coupled with advocacy for physical education itself (within your school and district) will help you in developing MbP. Keep records to show the changes you have made and advocate for your program with the various stakeholders who have an interest in what happens in physical education.

An invitation

We are, collectively and individually, interested in your experiences of using MbP. We have dedicated more than 40 years between us to researching pedagogical models and MbP and want to know more about how both are being used in practice. We currently know only what has been published in books and journals and know that there is much more work going on in this field. We have doctoral, masters and undergraduate students who want to study MbP and it would be fantastic to get you involved. In many respects we are engaged in advocacy and need to better understand and document evidence-based practice. We can be contacted at A.J.B.Casey@lboro.ac.uk and david.kirk@strath.ac.uk, respectively. Please let us know how you get on with the ideas in this book and tell us how we can help going forward.

We hope you get something out of this book and that you will try applying Models-based Practice in physical education, because without you and your efforts, MbP remains a hope and not a happening.

Reference

Kirk, D. (2013). Educational value and models-based practice in physical education. *Educational Philosophy and Theory*, *45*(9), 973–986.

Index

Note: Page locators in *italics* indicate a figure on the corresponding page.

accountability 16, *38*, 53
activist model: concept 19; methods 20, 41, 57; practice architecture 30, *36*
Aggerholm, Kenneth 21
Arendt, Hannah 21
aspirations: identification 9–11; limited 6; for pedagogical change 28–29; for student learning 7, 16; *see also* learning aspirations
assessment: curriculum and 2, 7, 9, 12, 28, 30, 71
Association for Physical Education (afPE) 56
Australian Council for Health, Physical Education and Recreation (ACHPER) 56

Bain, Linda 3, 8–9
Baker, Kellie 51
Baptista, João 18
Barker, Dean 21
Bowler, Mark 20–21

capitalised models 1–2
Casey, Ashley 16–19, 27, 29, 41, 46, 49–50, 53, 55, 57–59, 62, 64, 68–69
communication skills 16, 20, 37, *38*, 40, 65
conceptual framework (CF) model *7*, *8*, 14, 20

cooperative learning: concept 7, 12; model 1–2, 14, 16, 45, 53, 65; practice architecture *38*; principles and methods 22, 28, 30, 39–41, 44; reviews 18
critical participatory action research (CPAR) 66
curriculum: formulation 9, 12, 15, 19; models 3–4, 6–9, 14, 16, 19; multi-activity approach 5, 28, 41, 44, *45–46*, 49, 69, 71
Curriculum for Excellence (CfE) 6
Curtner-Smith, Matthew D. 29

Davies, Micheal 22
Dyson, Ben 3–4, 16

evidence-based practice 71, 73

face-to-face interaction 16, *38*
Fernandez-Rio, Javier 41
Flutter, Julia 57

Gard, Michael 6
Goodyear, Victoria A. 18
group: activity/activities 15–17, *34–35*, *38*; cooperation 39–41; development 39; persisting 11; processing 16, *38*, 40; recreation 56; stakeholders 65, 67

Harvey, Stephen 18
Hastie, Peter 18

HBPE *see* health-based physical education
health-based physical education/ health-based PE (HBPE): conceptual framework 20–21; cooperative learning model 1, 7; practice architecture 37, 42
Hellison, Don 17

individual accountability 16, 38, 40, 53
instructional models 3–4, 8, 14

Jarrett, Kendall 18
Jewett, Ann 3, 8–9
Johnson, David W. 16
Johnson, Roger T. 16

Kemmis, Stephen 66–68
Kirk, David 17–19, 66, 71

Larsson, Håkan 21
learning aspirations: learning to learn 29, 40, 57; levels 17, 35, 66; student centered 12, 16–17, 19–20, 34, 36, 65, 71
learning outcomes 9–12, 14, 21, 29–30
long game 27–28
Loughborough University 20
Lounsbery, Monica A.F. 5
Lund, Jacalyn 14

MacPhail, Ann 68–69
McKenzie, Thomas L. 5
McNeill, Katherine 10
Metzler, Michael W. *(Model-Based Instruction)* 3–4, 6, 8, 14
Models-based Practice (MbP): celebrating success 61; collaboration 19, 27, 45, 49, 52, 62, 66, 73; collective progress and feedback 45, 60, 67–68; focus on student learning 7, 12, 17, 22; getting started 42; making a case 62, 64, 66–68, 70; pedagogy 6, 11, 15–17, 41, 71; problem solving 54, 62; shared vision building process 50, 62, 73; terminology 3–4
Moderate to Vigorous Physical Activity (MVPA) 5–6, 41
Mosston, Muska 22
MVPA *see* Moderate to Vigorous Physical Activity

National Curriculum for Physical Education (NCPE) 6

O'Connor, Justen 59
Oliver, Kim 18–19

pedagogical model: design specifications 2, 9, 12, 69; five dominant themes 27; four elements of 2, 9–10, 23; groundwork 28; health-based 1, 20, 30, 55; multiple models 3–4, 69, 72; practice architecture 15, 31, 72; sequencing 44, 68; vulnerable youth 19; well-established 14, 24, 72; working with girls 18
pedagogy: definition 2; differences 41, 45–46; elements of 6–7, 9–10; role of teacher 15–16, 19–21
Physical and Health Education Canada (PHE Canada) 56
physical education: focus on content 6–7, 9, 12, 19–20; teaching 15 (*see also* TGfU); traditional 4
Physical Education of Ireland (PEAI) 56
Pill, Shane 22–23
positive interdependence 16, 38, 53
practice architecture: creation of 2–3; pre-designed nature 42–44, 46; shared vision development 50–51, 67, 71; structural characteristics 9, 11–12, 15, 72; *see also individual models*
practising model: exposure/use of 44; introduction of 1, 15; main idea 21, 30; practice architecture 32, 52
publications 18, 56

reconnaissance 47, 64, 66–67, 70
resources 2, 30, 43–44, 64, 66, 72
responsibility 16, 20, 53, 56; decision-making 17, 35; to self and others 38, 40, 44
Richards, Kevin A. 18
Rudduck, Jean 57

safety 15–16, 38, 40
Sallis, James F. 5
Sammon, Paul 20–21
Scottish Association of Teachers of Physical Education (SATPE) 56
Shriver, Victoria N. 18
Siedentop, Daryl 15, 29
skills: cognitive 4–6, 22; learning life skills 7, 17, 20, 35, 53; physical 42, 45, 49, 69; small group and interpersonal 16, 38, 40
Sloterdijk, Peter 21
Society for Health and Physical Education (SHAPE) 56
sport education: approaches to 1–4, 22, 65; architecture 33, 45.53.55; critical elements of 10, 14–15, 29; as non-negotiable 10–11; purpose of 41, 44
stakeholders 42, 65–67, 73
Standal, Øyvind 21
Stenhouse, Lawrence 3, 9

student: assessment 2, 7–10, 16–17, 19, 28, 30, 40–41, 68; communication skills 16, 20, 38, 40, 65, 67; interactions 16–17, 38, 40–41; involvement 15, 41, 56, 60, 69; student-centred teaching 12, 16, 19–20, 34, 36, 65
Suesee, Brendan 22–23

tactical games 14, 68
Tannehill, Deborah 14
teaching games for understanding (TGfU) 1–4, 7–8, 15–16, 30, 34
teaching personal and social responsibility (TPSR): pedagogy of affect 17; practicing model 30, 35, 53
teaching styles 10, 22–23, 31, 40
togetherness 16, 40
TPSR *see* teaching personal and social responsibility

Wallhead, Tristan 18
Williams, John 22
working with girls 18–19
World War II 4

youth 17, 18–20, 59

Zhao, Weili 28

For Product Safety Concerns and Information please contact our EU representative GPSR@taylorandfrancis.com
Taylor & Francis Verlag GmbH, Kaufingerstraße 24, 80331 München, Germany

www.ingramcontent.com/pod-product-compliance
Lightning Source LLC
Chambersburg PA
CBHW051759230426
43670CB00012B/2360